# Improve Your Profits . . .
# Satisfying Customers

# Improve Your Profits . . . Satisfying Customers

### Ron Sewell

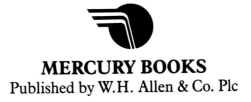

**MERCURY BOOKS**
Published by W.H. Allen & Co. Plc

First published in 1988
by the Mercury Books Division of
W.H. Allen & Co. Plc
44 Hill Street, London W1X 8LB

Cover Design and Artwork by Sandy Lawrence, No 1 Design & Print,
1 Queen Square, Bath
Set in 12/13 Plantin by Quadraset Ltd, Midsomer Norton, Avon
Printed and bound in Great Britain by Adlard & Son Ltd,
Letchworth, Herts


ISBN 1–85251–040–4

Also by Ron Sewell
*Building a Business*, Pan Books, 1986

# INTRODUCTION

I know that Ronald Sewell will not mind if I say that this book should not really have to be written. It is not simply Mr Sewell's direct prose style which makes you think 'Isn't this all rather obvious?' – it is also the message that is a truism, that the customer is king.

Sadly though, until recently, much of British business seemed to have forgotten the importance of that message – or at least to have failed to understand its significance. While we all worried about the price of British products and services, we did not pay the same attention to quality, design, marketing, after-sales service and all the other factors that make a company's products competitive in the fullest sense of that word.

Now, however, the tide is changing. The Enterprise Initiative, launched in January 1988 by DTI, seeks to direct more of companies' attention to these other factors, but it does so in a radically different climate.

As a nation, we are again discovering the pride of a job well done, and the stimulus of enterprise.

But there is still much to be done. I know that this book will be invaluable to businessmen who are prepared to ask themselves fundamental questions about the nature of their enterprise and it is in that spirit that I commend its message, for it is one that no company can afford to ignore.

**RT HON LORD YOUNG OF GRAFFHAM**
*April 1988*

---

'Having satisfied customers is the basis for profit enhancement – Ron Sewell's book clearly lays out a practical road map for achieving that goal.'

Buck Rodgers, author of *The IBM Way* and *Getting the Best Out of Yourself and Others*, published by Harper and Row.

# ACKNOWLEDGEMENTS

First, I must thank the Secretary of State for Trade and Industry, Lord Young, for the support of his masterly introduction. I would also like to thank all the individuals and organisations mentioned in this book. First, for the inspiration of the examples they provide and, second, for their courtesy in commenting on my references to them.

I am particularly grateful to Jan Carlzon of SAS who very kindly arranged for me to receive copies of his books and speeches, and to Frederick Polhill whose marvellous quarterly *Industrial Marketing Digest* provides a wealth of information on the ideas we have been discussing.

Finally, I owe a huge debt to my colleagues Sandy Lawrence, Tessa and Michael Crossfield for their help in every step of production, and to my publisher for being willing to produce a book on a subject I feel to be of critical importance for the growth both of individual companies and the British economy.

R.L. Sewell

# CONTENTS

# SUCCESS OR FAILURE

## WE ARE ALL CUSTOMERS . . .

Enjoyment of Shopping

We are all customers. Shopping is now Britain's main leisure activity! As individuals we know the way in which we like to be treated when we are customers. We want bright, cheerful, helpful individuals prepared to take the time and trouble to understand, and meet, our needs.

Evening Out

If we get bright, cheerful, and courteously attentive service from the waiter when we take our family out for a celebration meal, it adds to the enjoyment of the evening. We will leave a larger tip, and make a mental note to return to the restaurant in future. If the evening is spoilt by surly staff, reluctant to give us the attention we expect, the evening will be spoilt. We will be reluctant to leave a tip, and make a mental note never to go back to that restaurant again!

Success in Business

If we are in business, our success will depend on our ability to buy the right goods and services.

If we find a supplier, or a professional adviser, who puts himself or herself out to supply what we need, when and how we need it, and 'leans over backwards' to make sure we receive good service, we are pleased and grateful. Our workload is eased and we try to give that particular supplier as much business as possible. If we get rude or indifferent service, irregular deliveries, inaccurate paper work or find dealing with the supplier a stressful aggravation, then we do our best to find an alternative supplier.

What is the Problem?

We all know what we want as customers . . .

. . . just as we all know businesses which do not meet our needs.

Lack of Profit

Many businesses struggle along with unsatisfactory levels of profitability because they do NOT provide what customers want in the way they want it. Though they work hard to give a good service, they do not look at their business from their customers' point of view.

Increased Profits

So, by missing opportunities to 'add value' for their customers, they miss opportunities for increased profitability for themselves.

# PRODUCTS AND CUSTOMERS

## CONSIDER COMPUTERS

| | |
|---|---|
| Product Led | One man, brilliant technically, became preoccupied with striving to produce a technically advanced, highly innovative micro-computer. |
| Customer Driven | A second man researched customer needs, against competitive activities. He then set out to buy and assemble cost-effective components which enabled him to create, attract, satisfy, and retain customers at a price which customers found acceptable, but which gave him a profit large enough to expand his own business. |
| Question | Which man do you think deserved to succeed? |
| Outcome | The customer-orientated marketer, Alan Sugar, succeeded brilliantly, grew so fast that his company, Amstrad, was able to go public, and now his machines set industry standards in competition with IBM. |
| | The 'boffin' got himself into severe financial difficulties, primarily because he could not supply the right product at the right time, and eventually had to sell out that operation. |

## OVERWORKED AND UNDERPAID

| | |
|---|---|
| Thousands of Tragedies | It is a real tragedy for the individuals concerned – indeed for the British economy – that thousands of businesses have failed, are failing, and will fail because they are preoccupied with **WHAT** they do instead of **WHY** they should be doing it! |
| Small Scale: Individual Businesses | Individuals who start and run their own business do so because they are good at **doing**. They may be a highly qualified professional like an architect or accountant. They may be a skilled craftsman in wood, metal, or plastic. They may be gifted in their particular activity, be it computing or catering. |

But because they are preoccupied with:

- **What they do –**

instead of being preoccupied with:

- **What customers need and want** (and are prepared to pay for) –

they end up being 'overworked and underpaid' and fail to generate the profits they need to survive, let alone expand their business.

| | |
|---|---|
| Large-scale Industries | Executives who gain promotions steadily in a large organisation because they are brilliant technically or professionally, often struggle when they gain a senior appointment which gives them responsibility for the prime objective of the company, which is, or should be: |

**Satisfying customers profitably . . .**

| | |
|---|---|
| Product-led Executives | There are many British companies dominated by **'product-led'** executives, who have produced products based on what they want to produce . . . instead of what the customer needed. Whole industries have suffered in this way. In America the motor industry lost customers, and profits, because it failed to realise that customers would find smaller Japanese cars more suited to their needs. |

| | |
|---|---|
| Under-exploited Innovations | Similarly, the decline of the British motor industry was exemplified by the way in which Alec Issigonis, another brilliant 'boffin', produced the uniquely innovative 'Mini' but failed to capitalise on its potential world-beating success by pricing and positioning it correctly in the market-place. By being concerned with the **'product'** instead of with the **'customer'** the vehicle was under-priced, did not make a significant profit contribution and merely created a new market-place which other more customer-orientated manufacturers exploited profitably. |

# KING COTTON OR KING CUSTOMER

As early as 1953 UK cotton mills were facing hard times.

| | |
|---|---|
| David Alliance | David Alliance had come to Britain from Iran at the age of seventeen with no money and very little knowledge of English. |

| | |
|---|---|
| Bought Bankrupt Mill | The mill he was buying supplies from, in Oswaldtwistle, Lancashire, was facing liquidation, so he borrowed £10,000 from a money-lender at 27% interest and set about reviving the business despite the rationalisation facing the cotton industry. |

3

| | |
|---|---|
| **Customers Put First** | His plan was to get closer to the customer; **to put the customer first**. He provided the products they needed, more efficiently. Against the trend in the industry, he made the mill profitable and this enabled him to buy other cotton mills as they, too, fell on hard times. With each of his acquisitions, his principles were the same – get closer to the customer. **King Customer** was taking over from, and succeeding, where **King Cotton** had failed. |
| **Meeting Customer Needs** | In 1963 he purchased a mail order catalogue company, J.D. Williams (now part of the N. Brown Group). To find out how the customers viewed his business, he went around on many evenings, knocking at doors, posing as a student wanting to learn about the mail order business. In the year ending February 1987, that same company made a profit contribution of £8.7 million to his group. |
| **Acquisitions** | For one who could make a mill profitable, Lancashire was a land of opportunities. He started to buy businesses, Spirella and Vantona were among the first. In 1983 he bought Carrington Viyella which had lost £85 million in the previous three years. Within six months it was making a contribution to group profits. Within three years, turnover had been boosted from £103 million to £675 million, which included The Nottingham Manufacturing Company which was acquired in August 1985. This was a production-led company where heavy investment in plant meant great efficiency. |
| **£700 Million Underwriting** | In March 1986 he was able to buy Coats Patons, raising the £700 million underwriting he required in the City in a matter of hours. This was as a result of him previously explaining personally to analysts and bankers why he had faith, when others had none, that the British textile industry could compete. With Coats Viyella he now runs a £1.75 billion company with factories in more than thirty countries. |
| **Vision** | He is now regarded as a 'visionary' and vision is a very important word in any business. |
| **Customer Orientated a Success Formula** | When he acquired J.D. Williams it had a turnover of £2 million. By careful data-processing to analyse **what customers wanted to buy**, he was able to produce products which stood out in the minds of the customers at which they were aimed. (The technical name for this is 'product differentiation', to which we will return.) He then made sure, by tight stock control, that the products were available when |

ordered by customers. He also made sure that customers knew they were available by heavy investment in advertising. As a result, the company – now part of the N. Brown Group – increased its turnover from £2 million to over £75 million by 1987.

| | |
|---|---|
| **Delegation** | In his earlier take-overs, David Alliance split his purchases into smaller units and let the managers run the companies. As he explained in an interview, 'not all managers have to be brilliant, or intellectually motivated. If they enjoy what they are doing and find out **what the customers want**, they will do the job well.' |
| **Morale** | With this philosophy of independence for managers and a minimum of overheads at the centre, David Alliance recognises his reliance on people. He regards morale as important, and spends a high proportion of his time in finding the right people. Once hired, he believes in giving personal assistance in decision making, where required, and making his managers feel wanted. |
| **Standards** | Like Marks and Spencer, his concern for human relations extends down through the business. 'Why should I expect other people to work in conditions I would not tolerate myself?' he asked. As a result, he has always kept the unions on his side. |
| **King Cotton** | It is worth making the point again. The Lancashire cotton industry had been almost arrogant in its **preoccupation** with its **product**, exemplified with its worship of 'King Cotton'. As a result, it was facing almost irrevocable decline as new, low-cost producers stole the market 'from under their noses'. The same has been true of many other long-established British businesses. You can doubtless think of many examples yourself. |
| **Or King Customer?** | David Alliance, by **putting the customer first**, by personally banging on doors to ask them what they wanted, has brilliantly reversed that trend. While he is certainly a shining example who has succeeded in the most difficult of industries, he is not alone. |

# SALES-DRIVEN OR CUSTOMER-DRIVEN?

## RETRENCH OR GROW?

Distribution

Companies using trucks and vans to deliver and collect goods went through a very difficult period when the recession hit British Industry.

Most of the long-established companies had to rationalise their operations to survive. They had to cut costs and adapt their operations to meet tighter, more competitive conditions.

## MESSENGER TO MILLIONAIRE

Richard
Gabriel

In 1980, Richard Gabriel was a motorcycle messenger. Now he is a millionaire, with his company, Interlink, publicly listed. Interlink is now one of the largest overnight parcel delivery services in Britain.

Why?

So why has Richard Gabriel succeeded in an activity in which far too many competitors fight for market share? Indeed, most of the established companies had been watching their profit margins shrink as they chased more business, at lower margins; just like many other trades and industries.

# CUSTOMER-DRIVEN

Analysing
Customer
Needs

Richard Gabriel succeeded because he was prepared to adopt a **customer-driven** approach, rather than the sales-driven approach of his competitors. He admits that he had the advantage of starting a new business which could be designed to meet the needs of customers from scratch. Most of his competitors had to cut costs, reorganise, and alter their method of operations to meet changing conditions. But, he had the disadvantage of trying to gain a foothold, whereas they were well known, and long-established. Despite this disadvantage, he succeeded because:

- **He analysed the NEEDS of his CUSTOMERS, and worked out the most cost-effective way of MEETING THEIR NEEDS.**

Analysing
**Competitors**

When he first considered moving into distribution, it was clear that the market was overcrowded with competitors. So, he very carefully analysed the **strengths** and **weaknesses** of each competitor, together with the opportunities and the threats they faced before deciding on his own strategies.

Target
Customers

Rather than trying to be all things to all men, he selected a particular **group** of customers to serve.

**Creating**
a Service

He then set out to find a way of providing a service customers both needed and wanted. He recognised that the market was so cut-throat there was no customer loyalty. Efficiency was paramount. When you or I send a parcel, we want to make sure that it is collected from us on time, and is delivered within the time span promised. So, Richard Gabriel created a service to meet customer needs. For example, he designed his own computer system which, with the introduction of bar coding, enabled him to achieve a 99.8 per cent efficiency rate in the delivery of parcels to customers; which is what customers are buying.

Customer
Commitment

He also created a structure, based on franchising, which ensured that those doing the collection and delivery were equally committed to customer satisfaction.

# RESULT: SUCCESS

Richard Gabriel entered a highly competitive market-place, from which other companies were withdrawing. Many long-established competitors were introverted: they were looking inward at themselves, seeking to rationalise and to find ways of cutting costs.

Richard Gabriel looked outwards, he set out to satisfy customers by meeting customer needs. He succeeded brilliantly, when so many were failing, by:

- **Putting Customers First.**

---

### A Long-standing Problem

At the end of the nineteenth century, it was said that Britain was losing out to Germany because the Germans gave customers what they wanted. One book that popularised this viewpoint was by Ernest Williams who in 1896 wrote:

**'. . . The last thing an English firm usually considers when soliciting orders is the tastes of its customers. "These are our goods: take them or leave them", is in effect the general message . . .'**

Quoted by John O'Shaugnessy, *Competitive Marketing*.

# STARTING A BUSINESS FROM SCRATCH

## CHARLIE THE CRAFTSMAN

Building Your
Business

In *Building Your Business* (Pan Books) I wrote about 'Charlie the Craftsman' to give a story typical of the problems of those who start their own business.

Recipe for
Disaster

Charlie was a mechanic who started his own workshop. Because he was good, he was overloaded with work; which he under-priced! Because he was so busy working 'productively', he did not control the mechanics he recruited to help him, nor did he keep his books and invoicing up to date! As a result, he ran up a large overdraft and nearly went bankrupt. With the help of a new accountant, he survived. But it took him a long time to repay the overdraft and work became a 'grind' instead of a pleasure. His marriage and health suffered. Eventually, he did establish a modestly successful business, but even then he was probably still 'overworked and underpaid'.

## TURNING THE CLOCK BACK!

Starting from
Scratch

Let us imagine that Charlie could 'turn the clock back' and start his business again from scratch. How should Charlie – or any other man or woman – start his business?

Ten Step Plan

Starting a customer-orientated business requires a ten-step plan which we will be discussing together in this book. Let us look at how these ten steps could be applied to Charlie's business, or your own.

# YOUR TEN STEPS TO . . . IMPROVED PROFITS . . . FROM SATISFYING CUSTOMERS

**1 ESTABLISH YOUR VISION** That you have a **VISION** of building a business based on ensuring that your 'customers come first'.

**2 ASSESS VIABILITY** That you **ASSESS** your market-place by a thorough understanding of all existing or potential customers and thus the viability/the volume of business you can gain.

**3 DISCOVER CUSTOMER NEEDS** That you **DISCOVER** the business you are really in by clarifying the tangible and intangible **BENEFITS** customers need.

**4 SUB-DIVIDE CUSTOMERS** That you **SUB-DIVIDE** your customers by grouping together those who have any similarities in common with each other.

**5 SELECT YOUR CUSTOMERS** That you **TARGET** those groups of customers whose similar needs and wants you can satisfy better than your competitors.

**6 YOUR MISSION STATEMENT FOR SUCCESS** That your **VISION** of satisfying customers is encapsulated in a **MISSION STATEMENT** which, together with your **CULTURE**, will be the foundation stone of your business.

**7 CREATE A CUSTOMER SATISFYING PRODUCT OR SERVICE** That you **CREATE** a product or service which meets the needs of your target customer groups better than your competitors.

**8 ATTRACT YOUR CUSTOMERS** That you **ATTRACT** an increasing number of customers.

**9 SATISFY YOUR CUSTOMERS** That you **SATISFY** your customers.

**10 RETAIN & UPGRADE YOUR CUSTOMERS** That you **RETAIN** your customers by **UPGRADING** the way in which you meet their developing needs and thus achieve your **VISION**.

C C F
Customers Come First
However it's put...

# STEP ONE: VISION

**David Alliance**    As we have seen, David Alliance is regarded as a 'visionary'. He had a vision of revitalising the British textile industry when so many others could only bemoan its decline.

**The Body Shop**    You will be aware of the dramatic success of 'The Body Shop'. This was due to the **vision** of Anita Roddick, ably supported by her husband. At a time when established cosmetics companies attempted to sell eternal, film-style youthful beauty to women of all ages, Anita Roddick promised to be:

- **the most honest cosmetic company around.**

**Vision**    Indeed, as we will see later in this book, the driving sense of 'vision' lies behind every successful business. Invariably, the vision is something very simple and straightforward.

**Examples**    For example, the owner of a corner shop can have a vision of being:

- **the most cheerful, helpful, and enjoyable shop in the area.**

A professional accountant, instead of viewing his job as the preparation of accounts to meet statutory and tax requirements, can have a vision of:

- **improving clients' profitability.**

The owner of a restaurant, instead of feeling that he or she is in the food production business could have a vision of:

- **creating a thoroughly enjoyable 'occasion'.**

In other words, the focus is not on the mechanics of what a business does, but on the tangible and intangible benefits that customers derive from their contact with the business.

**Charlie's Vision**    So, what do you feel should be the vision of Charlie? For a start, like any vision, it must reflect his basic strengths. It must also be compatible with his values and life-style.

Charlie was a good craftsman, concerned with getting things right 'first time'. He wanted to be his own boss, but did not want all the hassles of running a business. He loved his wife and family, and was not prepared to become a 'workaholic'.

At the same time he derived maximum satisfaction from building a personal relationship with his customers, and their cars, and in exercising his unique skills in diagnosing, correcting, and tuning cars so that they ran sweetly. So, his vision statement would have been:

- **to provide the most honest and reliable tuning and preventative maintenance service for motorists in the area.**

# STEP TWO: ASSESS VIABILITY

Blind Faith

Many individuals who start their own business seem to have a 'blind faith' that there will be enough customers willing to buy from them, to make the business worthwhile. As we will see later, this is not always true. Even if there are enough customers to get the business going, there may not be enough customers to ensure that it has healthy, profitable growth.

Able and Willing to Buy

The existence of thousands of customers is no guarantee that they will be able, and willing to buy. It is vital for any businessman or woman to understand all the direct and indirect influences affecting customers both now, and in the future.

Test Market

By going to his local reference library, Charlie can find out that the total number of vehicles in use in his area is 3,374. But, few of the vehicles would come to Charlie. Let us study some of the influences which affect his potential market.

Factors Influencing Market

New cars are sold with a manufacturer's guarantee which requires the car to be serviced by a dealer holding that franchise. In general, manufacturers are extending the guarantee period to retain customers within the franchise network. Thus, Volvo gives a commitment to lifetime care on its vehicles.

A high proportion of new cars are bought by large organisations who specify the way in which the company vehicles will be serviced and maintained.

A significant proportion of cars are bought on 'contract maintenance' which locks the user into having the vehicle serviced and maintained on a predetermined basis.

| | |
|---|---|
| Marginal Motorists | When private individuals buy a new or used car, they often do so on very tight budgets, and are reluctant to spend money on servicing or maintenance. As a result many go to specialists who appear to be selling on price. |
| Non-customers | In short a high proportion of owners or drivers of vehicles in his area are very unlikely to become Charlie's customers. |
| Future Trends | What trends of the future may affect Charlie's business? Manufacturers are extending their periods of guarantee. Service intervals are being both extended, and servicing times reduced. |
| Growth of Technology | Increasingly, cars are becoming far more electronically controlled. Computerised diagnostic equipment is necessary to maintain them at peak levels of performance. |
| | Traditional materials are being replaced by plastic and even ceramics. Charlie, like every other business executive, needs to be aware of the influences in his market-place. |
| | He also needs to be aware of indirect influences affecting customers. |
| Customer Attitudes | Paradoxically, the more leisure time we have, the more reluctant we are to waste it and speed of service becomes increasingly valuable. The more that customers come to rely on their vehicles, the greater their unwillingness to be deprived of their use. |
| Dead End or Opportunity? | If Charlie is prepared to drift into the 'dead end' of being a 'backyard repairer' earning little more than he would do as an employee (but with a great deal more hassle), then assessing the viability of his market-place, and the factors likely to influence its future are a waste of time. |
| | If Charlie wants to build a business which will show him an acceptable standard of living, with a secure future, then studying the market-place in this way will turn out to be a good investment. |

## STEP THREE: CUSTOMER NEEDS

| | |
|---|---|
| Discover | Next Charlie has to discover the real needs and wants of his potential customers, how these needs are being met at present by existing organisations, and how they might be met in the future. |

| Speed, Convenience, Simplicity, Reassurance | Numerous organisations have published reports on how motorists view servicing. These indicate that motorists want speed, convenience, simplicity, and reassurance. Also, they are being conditioned by organisations like M & S to expect high standards of cleanliness in waiting and reception areas. Some successful dealerships now provide business executives with office-standard waiting rooms with phones or telexes on which they can work while their car is being repaired. |
|---|---|
| Technology | The increasing electronic content of vehicles will mean that he will need to generate a high enough level of profitability to buy each development in electronic testing equipment. |

## STEP FOUR: SUB-DIVIDE CUSTOMERS

| Diverse Backgrounds and Needs | It is old-fashioned common sense to recognise variations between customers. They differ by age, sex, ethnic origin, income levels, educational standards, type of work they do, type of leisure activities, type of home in which they live, and many other variants. |
|---|---|
| | What is less common is for business executives to consciously seek to turn this information to their advantage. |
| Success Factor | Companies who gain a competitive advantage do so because of the skill in which they sub-divide the market-place into distinct customer groups, a point to which we will return. |
| Grouping Charlie's Customers | As a result of studying his market-place, Charlie has recognised the following distinct groups: |

- **Company Cars**, where the organisation provides and services a car for its executives and employees.
- **Assisted Purchase**, where the owner or senior executives of a small company, professional practice, or other local business buy and run the car 'on the business' but need to organise the servicing and maintenance of the car themselves.
- **Quality Cars**, owned privately by wealthy individuals.
- **Second Cars** (and third cars). New or nearly new quality cars within a high income family, normally used primarily by the wife, and the teenage children.

- **Enthusiasts**, probably relatively well off young adults who are fanatically keen on driving a fast, highly-tuned car, able to make second-splitting starts from traffic lights!

The way in which potential car-owning customers can be grouped is endless. It can range from a hard-up student running a 'banger' to the old age pensioner striving to maintain personal mobility on a tight budget. (D.C. Cook is one dealership group offering special motoring plans to pensioners as a result!)

# STEP FIVE: SELECT YOUR CUSTOMERS

Targeting
Customers

You are more likely to gain a competitive advantage, and be able to satisfy your customers at an improved profit margin, if you select specific groups of customers whose similar needs and wants you can satisfy better than your competitors.

Selecting
Charlie's
Customers

The skill with which Charlie, or any other business executive, selects particular groups of customers will determine his business success or failure.

It is likely that three particular groups of people could be his target:

- **Senior Executives** from business and professions who enjoy top-class motoring but are reluctant to spend their time on 'managing' their vehicles.

- **The wives** (and possibly children) of these business and professional executives who are keen to ensure that their families have safe, reliable transportation.

- **Younger men and women** who are 'fanatics' about fine-tuning. (Perhaps those involved in motor racing or rallying.)

# STEP SIX: MISSION AND CULTURE

Achieving
Vision

Having carried out Steps Two, Three, Four, and Five, it is now possible to write down a statement explaining how Charlie's vision will be achieved.

Foundation
Stone of
Success

This is known as a **'mission statement'**, which serves as the foundation stone of the business thereafter.

It should have five elements:

- the customers to be served

- the customer needs to be met

- the way in which these needs will be met

- the **culture** which will motivate employees to meet customer needs

- the physical and financial resources needed.

Charlie's Statement

So, what do you think should be Charlie's 'mission statement'?

Bear in mind that it should be the most crucially important statement made for any business. (Some progressive companies have their mission statement boldly displayed at the entrance to their office or factory.)

So, perhaps Charlie could decide to polish up a mission statement on the following lines:

---

**Charlie's Mission Statement**

To select, attract, satisfy, and retain a limited number of motorists prepared to pay a premium price for a highly personalised 'vehicle management service' which maintains and tunes vehicles for optimum safety, reliability, and performance.

To provide this service by investing appropriately in spotlessly clean but well equipped work bays. To ensure that vehicles are valeted inside and out before being returned to customers. To provide a detailed report on the condition of the vehicle, and an equally open and detailed invoice for the work carried out.

To provide this service with total integrity, openness, helpfulness, and – above all – cheerfulness, which will add to the pleasure and reassurance which customers obtain from the private and business use of their vehicles. To generate the profits needed to maintain these standards.

---

The importance of this statement lies in the commitment which Charlie is making to customers: the service he intends to provide; and the way in which he intends to set out to provide it.

# STEP SEVEN: CREATING A CUSTOMER SATISFYING SERVICE

**Customer Needs and Wants**

What are the real needs and wants of the three groups of customers Charlie has targeted?

What do you think they are?

Most executives, under today's highly competitive conditions, are forced to become 'workaholics'. Their car is important to them, both as a prestige symbol, and as a way of making money by being able to drive to and from business appointments.

If they could 'wave a magic wand' they would like to be able to get in a smart, clean car which would start first time without fail and be maintained in a manner which ensured that it never let them down.

Similarly, their wives will want a clean car which will never let them down as they go shopping, or collecting the children from school.

**Creating the Service**

What service do these two groups of customers want?

Perhaps a personal car management service which, among other things, would undertake to:

- Valet the car regularly both inside and out, to ensure that it is always in pristine condition.

- A safety service which will ensure that tyres are always at the right pressure, and well within legal conditions, that brake fluids, and all similar essential safety and performance indicators, are operating at required levels of performance.

- A 'franchise service' which will ensure that the vehicle is taken to the franchise dealership for the services required to comply with the manufacturers' warranties.

- A preventative maintenance service which will do whatever is necessary to ensure that the car is always in perfect running order.

- A collection and delivery service based on 'servicing by appointment' so that, instead of having to part with your vehicle for a complete day, you know that if Charlie gets the vehicle by 3.30 pm, you can have it back at 5.30 pm. Or, that if you give Charlie the vehicle at 5.30 pm when you finish work, you can have it back at 7.30 pm before you go out for dinner!

- A 'management service' which will maintain, probably on a micro-computer, complete details as to the cost of running

17

the vehicle – mileage driven, cost of petrol, cost of repairs, estimated depreciation, and even (if required for tax purposes) a projected split between personal and business mileage so that the cost-conscious business executive can see the true cost of his motoring.

## Satisfying 'Fanatics'

The only service that the 'fanatics' would want is top-flight tuning, by appointment, probably on a basis which enables them to be involved in what is going on!

## Providing the Service

If you refer back to Charlie's mission statement, what other implications are there in regard to the way in which Charlie should run his business?

## Personal Service

First, Charlie has promised to provide a friendly, helpful, personal service. He will need to ensure that he has an extrovert, outgoing approach to customers, and always wears smart, clean clothes.

If he employs anyone to help him, particularly with his 'collection and delivery' service, then that person also needs to be very cheerful, helpful, and friendly, and to be equally clean and smart in appearance.

## Facilities

In his mission statement he has committed himself to create the ambience appropriate to handling highly prized cars for 'up-market' individuals. This implies that he will need a very modern looking workshop, always spotlessly clean, with all the appropriate advanced technological equipment.

The implications of a 'collect and delivery' service may be that his customers rarely visit him, but, when they do, they should have a carpeted waiting room, with high quality comfortable chairs, appropriate 'up-market' newspapers and magazines, and – if necessary – access to business telephones. If the wives of his customers visit him, appropriate magazines of interest to women and an ultra-clean washroom would be essential.

## Systems

Finally, the commitment Charlie is making implies that he will **position** his operation so that every activity reinforces his **mission**. This will include a micro-computer able to store detailed records on every customer, with precise details on what has been done, and what needs to be done on their vehicle. If the vehicle management service proves viable, it will also need to keep detailed operational costs. The computer would also be able to do invoicing and to produce very personal letters to all Charlie's customers.

Test Marketing — Jan Carlzon – who brilliantly turned around three Swedish businesses including SAS – tells the story of how they set out to design a tour package for elderly people in Sweden. To their chagrin, when they did some test marketing, they found that the last thing these potential customers wanted was to be grouped together as if they were 'geriatrics'. They wanted to mix with younger people because they still regarded themselves as young!

So too should Charlie do some test marketing to ensure that he is really meeting the true needs and wants of his target customers. Like David Alliance, he may need to go around, knocking on doors, not seeking to sell (except insofar as he will be selling himself) but to find out what customers want; . . . and are prepared to pay for!

## STEP EIGHT: ATTRACT YOUR CUSTOMERS

Marketing Platform — Next, how does Charlie attract the potential premium customers he has targeted?

He has started by creating what might be called a 'marketing platform'. He has **positioned** himself to provide a very personal, highly skilled, totally comprehensive service from highly equipped, quality facilities. To build on this **position**, he needs to ensure that everything he does reinforces the **perception** he wishes his customers to have of him.

Image — Thus, the design of his letterheading needs to create the right perception, as do his own trade vehicles.

19

| Leaflet Drop | If he knows his locality well, he should know the areas of the town in which the older, wealthier, private motorists are likely to live. (For a modest sum he can buy a copy of the Electoral Register to get the names of the individuals living in these areas.) So, he might consider arranging for an attractively prepared letter/leaflet to be delivered to these houses.

The Yellow Pages would give him the names and addresses of local doctors, dentists, solicitors, accountants, and other professionals. An hour or two in the local reference library should – with the friendly help available from most librarians – furnish him with the names of local businesses and their senior executives. (A directory such as 'Kompass' does this.) |

**...n Plant & ...nstruct. Co. (Hldgs) Ltd,**
King Road Avenue, Avonmouth,
  Bristol BS11 9HG (Tel. Avonmouth823333)
**Bank:** Lloyds. Avonmouth
**Office Hours:** M-F 8-6
**Loc:** Adjacent Port Authority Offices
**Directors:** D.H.N.Squires (Ch), D.A.Johnson
  (Group MD)
**Co Reg No:** 499947
**No. Employees:** 90

**... & Co. Ltd**
**...urs:** M-F 8-6
**...oc:** Near Chittenden Industrial Estate
**Directors:** J.G.Ford (MD), J.B.Hornby (Comm)
**Share Cap:** Subsidiary of Kato Cranes (Ltd)
**No. Employees:** 10
**Product Groups:** 40

**Anstee & Ware Ltd,**
Avonmouth Way, Avonmouth BS11 9HE
  (Tel. Avonmouth(0272)823501)
**Telex:** 444109
**Bank:** National Westminster
**Office Hours:** M-F 9-5
**Loc:** Off M5 at juctn 18
**Directors:** G.H.Anstee (Ch), J.W.Anstee (MD),
  V.C.Ware (Sec), M.Trigg (Electrical), F.J.Padden
  (Engineering)
**Executives:** M.E.Fry (Gen Eng Mgr), P.Ryder
  (Works Electrical Mgr)
**Share Cap:** Authorised £100,000 Issued
  £97,000
**Co Reg No:** 477097 Tu...
**No. Employees:** ...
**Product G...**

**Barlow Handling Ltd, Branch**
Second Way, Avonmouth Way, Avonmouth,
  Bristol BS11 8DF
  (Tel. Avonmouth(0272)821461)
**Telex:** 449908
**For full details see:** Maidenhead, Berks...

† **The Be...**
**Ru...**

| Direct Mail | Given that the Post Office has concessionary schemes to encourage young businesses to use direct mail, it could be cost-effective for Charlie to draft a direct-mail letter and – using his word processor/ computer – to send personally addressed and signed letters to all the business executives, professionals, and private motorists he has identified. If he has problems in writing a direct-mail letter, a local agency, or even a journalist on the local newspaper, may be able to help him. |

| Press Interest | In fact, he could invite the motoring correspondent of his local newspaper to see his new facility in the hope that he will so impressed with its uniqueness that he will write a story about it. |

| News Story | To give the local newspaper a 'hook' on which to write such a story, he could invite an influential local businessman, the Mayor, or even the local Beauty Queen to officially open his new premises. |
|---|---|
| Promotion | As an opening promotion, he could invite the local motoring club to his new premises, for a demonstration of modern tuning techniques. |
| Presentations | He could get a local agency to produce a slide/cassette presentation on the advantages of his comprehensive private car management service and seek opportunities to give this presentation at meetings of local clubs such as Round Table, Rotary, and Women's Guilds, or even take it into the boardroom of local companies. If he feels inarticulate, it could be possible to hire someone to do it for him. If he could find a local 'personality' to do so, so much the better. |

## STEP NINE: SATISFY CUSTOMERS

| Ultimate Test | The ultimate test by which every business stands or falls is the extent to which Charlie does succeed in satisfying customers.

He, like every other business, needs a **'customer-satisfaction index'**.

Ideally Charlie – or his wife – needs to ring up each customer after he has worked on their vehicles to make sure that they were completely satisfied.

He could have the occasional 'Cheese and Wine' party for his customers to discuss, on a group basis, the extent to which he is succeeding in meeting customer needs.

(He might get the local motoring correspondent to do an independent study on the extent to which Charlie satisfies his customers in relation to his competitors!)

If, for any reason, he loses a customer, he needs to work very hard to investigate and resolve any source of complaint. Often, the best advertisement for a business is an initially dissatisfied customer who had his complaint resolved promptly and fairly. |
|---|---|

## STEP TEN: RETAIN

| Retention Index | Finally, Charlie needs to ensure that he retains all his customers, by a specific programme of activities. He needs to find a yardstick by which he can measure his **'customer-retention index'**. |
|---|---|

| | |
|---|---|
| Computer Records | His micro-computer should be programmed to highlight – based on the average weekly mileage of the customer concerned – when next each customer's vehicle will need attention. Charlie should then send an attractively printed postcard or even a personally signed letter to each customer as a reminder. If the customer does not bring his vehicle in, Charlie, his wife, or an assistant, should ring to find out why. |
| Building Relationships | Charlie, like every other business executive, should seek to build a long-standing relationship with his customers. If when reading the newspapers or magazines he sees some particularly interesting item which may relate to them, the business they run, or the model of the car they own, he can send them a photocopy of the clipping 'with compliments'. |
| 'Owners' Club' | He might even form a 'club' for his customers and organise the occasional semi-social meeting with a film show or guest speaker. |
| | Women are becoming an increasingly important section of motorists. More than 30 per cent of cars are bought by women in their own right; apart from the very direct influence they have on the purchase of a family car. So, Charlie might organise the occasional 'club' meeting for women related to their particular needs and interests. |
| Upgrading Service | Charlie will need to review regularly every aspect of this Ten Step Plan so that he is better able to meet the ever-changing needs and expectations of his customers by **upgrading** the way in which he achieves his **vision**. |

## SATISFYING CUSTOMERS . . . PROFITABLY

| | |
|---|---|
| Competitor Pricing | When Charlie assessed the strengths and weaknesses of his competitors (Step Five), he found that most of the quality service departments in the area charged customers between £18 and £20 an hour for a somewhat impersonal service. (This compared very favourably with the £30 or £50 an hour charged by washing machine mechanics!) However, his competitors' customers had to deliver and collect their own vehicles; were not able to talk to the mechanic who worked on their vehicle – but had to rely on the interpretation of a receptionist; and had to leave their vehicles all day in the hope that the garage could 'fit it in'. |

| | |
|---|---|
| Customers' Reactions | Charlie found a young marketing student who needed to do a project as part of his diploma course. Charlie got him to design a short 'perception analysis' questionnaire, and to go out into the streets and car parks of the town to ask motorists their perceptions of local garages. |
| | The **'perception'** relating to some of his competitors was that – because they were on individual incentive schemes – mechanics were preoccupied with earning a bonus to the detriment of quality. |
| | There was also a reaction against the manner in which some of the competitors prepared their invoices. |
| Price Benefit Analysis | So, Charlie concludes that for his: |

- 'Right first time' service
- in first-class conditions
- with total integrity and openness
- with detailed vehicle records and analysis, and, above all,
- his cheerfulness and helpfulness to customers
- **he could charge £24 an hour.**

Test marketing among pilot customers proved that this was an acceptable charge. Indeed some customers indicated that they would be willing to pay Charlie an annual retainer to take their vehicle management worries away from them.

Obviously valeting services would be charged on a different basis.

| | |
|---|---|
| Profit Potential | With one or two trainees to improve his own productivity (while still receiving genuine training) he could probably earn at a rate in excess of £50,000 a year. |
| | This level of income, on relatively low overheads, would quickly enable him to repay his development costs, sustain his investment in improvements, have a very pleasant life-style, and still have money to put into his personal pension plan. |
| Contrast | Contrast this case study on what Charlie should have done, against what he actually did. Like so many others who start their own business, he only charged his customers £7 an hour. He worked far too long, far too hard, had no **vision**, and nearly destroyed himself, and his marriage! |

# EVERY BUSINESS

These principles apply to every business, to every shop, trade, profession, or industry; or even charity.

David Alliance applied them when building his international £1.75 billion textile business from his initial £8,000 loan.

Richard Gabriel with Interlink, and Anita Roddick with The Body Shop also followed the same principles.

**Everyone running a business, large or small, can improve satisfaction, and thus increase profits, if they take the time and trouble to be totally professional in working through the Ten Step Plan so that – by doing the basics exceptionally well – they gain a competitive advantage.**

# OVERCOMING BARRIERS TO GROWTH

## THE REALITY OF BUSINESS

Individuals

An increasing number of men and women are starting their own businesses. Most are preoccupied with trying to earn money from what **'they do'**. If they were to spend time to think about the **'needs and wants'** of their customers, they would be able to achieve greater customer satisfaction with enhanced profits.

Small
Companies

Individuals who are prepared to work hard enough, long enough, can achieve the first stage of growth in their company. They can generate enough business to justify employing a team of employees and supervisors to meet the needs of a limited number of customers.

Second-stage
Growth

Most companies face problems as they strive to achieve 'second-stage' growth. This means that the business will cease to be totally dependent on the owner but can afford a team of managers/directors, and can generate the finance needed to place the entire business on a sound footing with adequate resources. The problem is to gain the significant increase in the number of customers needed to cover this steep jump in overheads.

The company will need to become far more effective in the way in which it sets out to identify, attract, satisfy, and retain customers. Unless it can do so, it will not gain the financial support it needs.

Larger
Companies

During the recession you will have read of many companies which were forced into liquidation. Some were once famous household names. Invariably, they were **'product-led'** companies which could not respond quickly enough to the changing and increasingly competitive environment.

# LIFECYCLE OF INDUSTRY

Cradle to Grave  As human beings, we are familiar with the cycle of life. We are born, grow up, mature, age, and – sadly – die. Industries go through the same process, as illustrated in the diagram below.

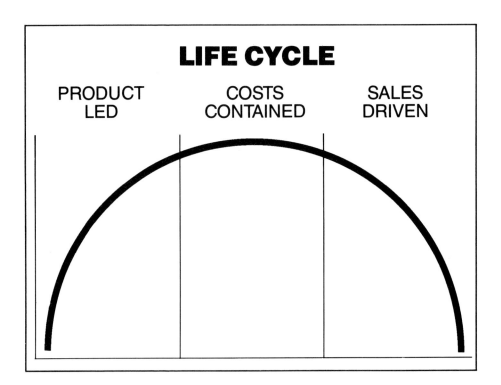

# TECHNOLOGY TO INSOLVENCY

Technology  Industries, too, can start, grow, mature, decline, and die.

In the birth phase of an industry, the dominant executives tend to be those with technical expertise of producing a new product, or service, and thus we talk of an industry being **'product-led'**.

Costs
Constrained  As an industry starts to mature, it needs to consolidate and control costs. This phase sees the arrival of financially orientated chief executives. During this phase, we talk of an industry, or a trade, being **'cost-constrained'**.

Taken to extremes, cost-cutting can kill a company, or an industry. So, as an industry 'matures', it becomes very concerned to cover costs by increasing sales.

| | |
|---|---|
| Sales-driven | It becomes **'sales-driven'**. But, by now, the industry is highly competitive, and additional sales can only be achieved by discount, special promotions, and other gimmicks which – apart from devaluing the product and the company – reduces the margin of profitability to the point where sales need to be doubled . . . just to stand still! In fact, since everyone is trying to double their own sales, they all go bankrupt together! |
| | If you lived through the recession of the 1970s and early 1980s, you can think of many examples of industries, and of companies, which have gone through this cycle; particularly when facing the additional competition of imports from countries with lower costs. |

## TEN STEP PLAN

| | |
|---|---|
| Find a Need and Fill It | As we have seen, there is a solution to the problem. It is to find a customer need, and satisfy it . . . profitably by applying our Ten Step Plan. |
| Buck the Trend | Richard Gabriel created a new way of supplying an improved service to companies wanting their goods delivered. Coats-Viyella has achieved profits of £182 million to demonstrate that Britain can fight back against the cheap imports which devastated the textile industry in the late 1970s. |
| | How was this successful recovery achieved? Not by being product-led, cost-constrained, nor sales-driven; but by being totally customer-orientated, and applying the Ten Step Plan. |

## GETTING OUTSIDE YOUR BUSINESS

| | |
|---|---|
| Pram Shop | You have just been told that a long-lost uncle has died and left you his chain of pram shops in North London. Your delight quickly turns to gloom when you discover that they are losing money heavily. There are too many prams chasing too few customers. The only way to sell a pram is to discount it heavily. |
| Question | How would you use this situation to turn yourself into a millionaire? |
| | What did the prospective mother want as her pregnancy progressed? The last thing she needed was to go from shop to shop to look for all the things her baby would need toiletries, ointments and cotton wool, nappies, potties, clothes, and prams. Surely, she would much prefer the concept of 'one-stop shopping' where she could get all her requirements, in comfort, at one location . . . Mothercare! |

Mothercare This now highly successful group of shops was once a struggling chain of pram shops in North London.

Setting out to identify and satisfy customers' needs dramatically improved profitability and turned Selim Zhilka into a millionaire.

## CREATING A NEW LIFECYCLE

Case Studies Many other companies have been able to create a new lifecycle for themselves by changing their approach: by stopping thinking about **what** they do; and starting to think about **why** they do it.

They have started to base all their actions on our Ten Step Plan and, as a result, have improved their profits by . . . satisfying customers . . . profitably.

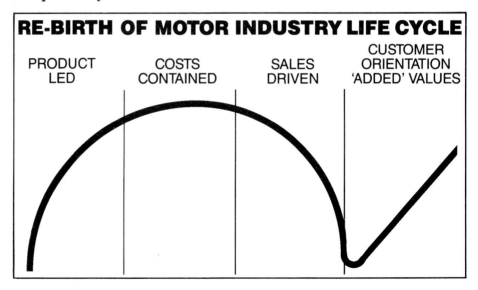

**RE-BIRTH OF MOTOR INDUSTRY LIFE CYCLE**

| PRODUCT LED | COSTS CONTAINED | SALES DRIVEN | CUSTOMER ORIENTATION 'ADDED' VALUES |

# STRATEGIC LEADERSHIP

European
Research

*The Winning Streak* quotes research by Professor Pupmin into thirty companies in German-speaking Europe.

Higher Profits

He found, as we have already seen in the case of Richard Gabriel, that even in a severely depressed, highly competitive industry, the few companies that shone with health were those which were totally customer-orientated. While the companies struggling for profitability, if not survival, tended to be those preoccupied with what they were doing and how much it cost them!

Extroverts and
Introverts

In fact, Professor Pupmin relates success and failure to the style of leadership.

Successful, customer-orientated companies tend to be led by extroverts who enjoy building relationships with people.

He claims that unsuccessful companies, preoccupied with product cost, tend to be led by introverted people who do not build the right customer relationships because of their innate shyness with people.

# CONCLUSION

Whether you are:

- Running your own company:

  or
- the chief executive of a large organisation, or the senior executive of one of its divisions or departments:

  or
- giving up your spare time to a voluntary organisation,

- you will be far more successful, have greater job satisfaction, and improve your profitability

  if:
- you **STOP** thinking about the product, service, or activity, and

- **START applying our Ten Step Plan to ensure total customer orientation.**

Bird's Eye
View

On the following pages you will see a slightly more detailed version of our 'bird's eye view'.

Let us just summarise the breakdown of each step.

# YOUR TEN STEPS TO ... IMPROVED PR⊘

## 1 ESTABLISH YOUR VISION
That you have a **VISION** of building your business by ensuring that your 'customers come first'.

## 2 ASSESS VIABILITY
That you **DEFINE** your market-place by a thorough understanding of all existing or potential customers, their total purchases, and thus the **VIABILITY** of the market share you seek to achieve.

Further, that you **UNDERSTAND** all the direct and indirect influences shaping the future size and **STRUCTURE** of your market-place.

## 3 DISCOVER CUSTOMER NEEDS
That you **DISCOVER** the business you are really in by clarifying the tangible and intangible **BENEFITS** customers need and want, including any unsatisfied wants; having regard to how these needs and wants are likely to change as society develops.

**C**
গ্রাহকদের
顧客
How⊘
Custom⊘

## 4 SUB-DIVIDE CUSTOMERS
That you **SUB-DIVIDE** your market-place by grouping together customers who have any similarities in common with each other.

## 5 SELECT YOUR CUSTOMERS
That you carry out a Strengths, Weaknesses, Opportunities and Threats Analysis of your company and its competitors to help you **TARGET** those groups of customers whose similar needs and wants you can satisfy better than your competitors.

# 'S . . . **FROM SATISFYING CUSTOMERS**

**10 RETAIN & UPGRADE YOUR CUSTOMERS**
That you **RETAIN** your customers by conscious retention policies the success of which is measured by your '**Customer Retention Index**', and that you continuously **UPGRADE** the way in which you meet customer needs and wants by keeping ahead of their expectations in a rapidly changing environment; and thus achieve your **VISION**.

**9 SATISFY YOUR CUSTOMERS**
That you **SATISFY** your customers by monitoring closely their reactions to the way in which you seek to meet their needs and wants through your own '**Customer Satisfaction Index**'.

**8 ATTRACT YOUR CUSTOMERS**
That you **ATTRACT** an increasing number of customers by the way in which you **POSITION** yourself to create the right **PERCEPTIONS** in the minds of your customers, and through a sustained programme of **PROMOTIONS** both to your direct customers, and those able to influence their decision to buy from you.

**7 CREATE A CUSTOMER SATISFYING PRODUCT OR SERVICE**
That you **CREATE** a product or service which meets the needs of your target customer groups better than your competitors through your competitive **STRATEGIES**, your **DESIGN**, your **ORGANISATION**, your communication **SYSTEMS** and your **CHANNELS** of distribution.

**6 YOUR MISSION STATEMENT FOR SUCCESS**
That your **VISION** of satisfying customers is encapsulated in a **MISSION STATEMENT** which — by stating the **CULTURE** you intend to build — will serve as the foundation stone of your business.

# YOUR TEN STEP PLAN

Step One    You need a **vision** of building a business by ensuring that your 'customers come first'.

Step Two    You need to **assess** the viability of your **vision** by:

- **Measuring** the size of your market-place by studying all existing or potential customers, their total purchases, and thus the viability of the share of the market-place you seek to achieve.

- **Understand** that you ensure that you have a deep understanding of all the direct and indirect influences affecting you, and your customers, both now and – more importantly – in the future as the pace of change quickens.

- **Structure.** That you thoroughly understand the 'structure' of your trade, industry, or profession and – again – the way in which this 'structure' may change in response to competitive pressures in the future.

Step Three
- **Discover.** That you discover the business you are really in by looking at what you do from the viewpoint of your customers.

- **Benefits.** That you understand the benefits which your customers are seeking to achieve in buying your product or service. Further that you use this understanding to discover any unsatisfied wants or needs of your customers at present so that you can better meet their needs both now, and in the future, as circumstances change.

Step Four    **Sub-divide your customers.** That you recognise the diverse natures of customers and seek to find creative ways of grouping customers with similar wants and needs together.

Step Five    **SWOT Analysis: Competitors.** That you carefully analyse the Strengths and Weaknesses of your competitors, and the particular Opportunities and Threats they face.

**SWOT Analyse: Your company.** Similarly, that you carry out an honest appraisal of your own Strengths and Weaknesses and the Opportunities and Threats that you face.

**Target.** Having done so, that you target those particular groups of customers whose similar needs and wants you can satisfy better than your competitors.

| | |
|---|---|
| Step Six | **Mission Statement.** That you encapsulate: |

- The customers you intend to serve.
- The customers' needs to be met.
- The way in which these needs will be met.
- The culture you will create for employees, suppliers, and customers, and
- Your profit objective.

This **mission statement** will serve as the foundation stone of your business thereafter.

**Culture.** The culture you create, primarily by your own example among employees, suppliers, and customers, will be the key factor in whether or not you achieve your **vision**.

| | |
|---|---|
| Step Seven | **Creating a customer-satisfying product or service.** This will involve a number of inter-related activities, as below: |

- **Strategic Leadership.** You will need a clearly defined strategy, in respect of the groups or segments of customers you intend to serve, based on choosing between:

  **Adding Value** and/or

  **Saving Costs.**

- **Design.** The way in which you design your product or service includes both the design of the product or service itself, and the way it is presented to your customers. For example, do you sell your product, or, do you rent out the use of your product?

- **Organisation.** Your commitment to 'putting customers first' and your work in designing your product or service will be wasted unless you recruit, train, and motivate customer-orientated employees who feel free to use their initiative in meeting customer needs because they have the right organisation behind them.

- **Systems.** A key element in good customer relations will be the systems you employ to make it easier for customers to order, receive, and pay for your goods and services.

- **Channels.** Will your customers acquire your products directly from you, or through intermediaries such as distributors, wholesalers, dealers, retailers, or franchisees? If so, your systems for recruiting, training, motivating, and controlling these **'channels'** will be a key element in how well you serve your 'end customers'.

- **Locations.** Whether you are running your own business through your own branches, or using third parties, **location** will be a key element in attracting and satisfying customers.

Step Eight **Attracting customers.** The key to your success in attracting your customers will depend on:

- **Position.** You will need to consciously think about how you 'create a window' in the mind of prospective and existing customers by correctly **positioning** everything you do.

- **Perceptions.** If you are successful in correctly positioning yourself, you will be able to create the right **perceptions** in the minds of existing and potential customers.

- **Promotions.** Creating the right **perceptions** will then make it easier to run cost-effective **promotions to attract customers**.

Step Nine **Satisfying your customers.** You need to ensure that you do **satisfy** your customers by monitoring closely their reactions to the way in which you seek to meet their needs and wants through your own:

- **Customer-satisfaction Index.**

Step Ten **Retain your customers by upgrading.**

- **Retain.** That you retain an increasing number of your customers by conscious customer retention policies, the success of which is measured by your:

  **Customer-retention Index.**

- **Upgrade.** That by consciously reviewing Steps Two, Three, Four, Five, Seven, Eight, and Nine you continuously **upgrade** the way in which you meet customer needs and wants by keeping ahead of their expectations in a rapidly changing environment; and thus achieve:

  Your **Vision.**

Putting it into Practice Having got this Ten Step Plan clearly in our minds, let's look at each step in turn in more detail.

# ESTABLISH YOUR VISION

That you have a **VISION** of building your business by ensuring that your 'customers come first'.

## THE 'HEART' OF YOUR BUSINESS

Your body cannot function without your heart. Equally, your business cannot function unless it has a 'heart' which finds expression in your **vision**.

You may be 'starting a business from scratch'.

You may have responsibility for maintaining the momentum of a long-established business.

Or, you may need to revive a business which has 'lost its way'.

In every case, you will need to start with a **vision**. Let us look at some examples.

## STARTING FROM SCRATCH

The Body Shop

On page 11 we discussed the dramatic success of The Body Shop, the 'heart' of which was the **vision** of Anita Roddick to build:

- **The most honest cosmetic company around,**

- and to 'bang the drum' to make sure that she communicated effectively her **vision** to the whole world.

David Alliance

To buy his first bankrupt cotton mill, David Alliance borrowed £8,000. Later he was able to borrow £700 million because he had **communicated** his **vision** of reviving the British textile industry to those whose support he needed.

Jaguar Cars

When Sir John Egan was revitalising Jaguar Cars, he set out what he was striving to achieve in one easily understandable **vision** from which everything followed. He ordained that the **vision** of Jaguar Cars was to:

- **'Make money by satisfying customers'.**

These were five very simple words, but they were hammered home to every one of his executives, employees, and suppliers at every level of his business. The outcome was a success story.

## LET'S GET IN THERE AND FIGHT

**Jan Carlzon and SAS**

In *Moments of Truth* Jan Carlzon described the way he revitalised the then loss-making SAS Airline. A key element in his strategy was to change employee attitudes. He ignited a radical change of **culture** at SAS. Traditionally, executives dealt with investments, management, and administration. Service was of secondary importance – the province of employees located way out on the periphery of the company.

**Communicating Vision**

He distributed a little red book entitled, 'Let's Get in There and Fight' to every one of his executives and employees. This gave in very concise terms, the **vision** he and his board were seeking to achieve. He writes:

'. . . by diffusing responsibility and communicating our **vision** to all employees we were making more demands on them. Anyone who is not given information cannot assume responsibility. But anyone who is cannot avoid assuming it. Once they understood our **vision**, our employees accepted responsibility enthusiastically which sparked numerous, simultaneous and energetic developments in the company'.

**The entire company – from the executive suite to the most remote check-in terminal – was focused on service.**

We are in bad shape. But we haven't reached the crisis point yet.
If we were, we wouldn't know how to get our nose up again.

But we can. If we are ready to fight for our jobs and our future, we can recover.

# MAINTAINING MOMENTUM

Serving the Community

The founder of Marks & Spencer, Michael Marks (like David Alliance) arrived in Britain barely able to speak English. He borrowed £5 to start his business; he probably did not think in terms of having a **vision**, but he did have a **dream** of serving his customers. Later, his grandson Lord Sieff expressed the **vision** of Marks & Spencer as being to:

- **Make a profit and serve the community.**

Undoubtedly, the reason for Marks & Spencer's distinctive success has been to demonstrate that efficiency and profitability are compatible with a deep human feeling for the needs and wants of those who serve it as employees, and those it serves as customers.

# STAYING AHEAD

Unigate

'It demands exceptional vision to sustain market leadership and achieve growth in a rapidly changing world. Unigate has that **vision**.

'By anticipating customer needs, Unigate continues to stay ahead of its competitors. The group invests in the future with confidence.

'Unigate's continued growth is based on effective corporate development. Strategic management has led to profitable operations, sound capital investment, and imaginative acquisitions.

'After five years of steady growth, 1987 has been another year of outstanding performance.'

John Clements, the Chairman of Unigate, believes that it does demand exceptional **vision** to sustain market leadership and achieve growth 'in an increasingly competitive world'.

In the past five years he has virtually doubled the return on trading capital 'employed' from 14.3 per cent to 28.3 per cent.

# FOUNDATION STONE OF SUCCESS

Deep Sense of Purpose

When we are talking about **vision**, we are talking about a deep sense of purpose: a philosophy, a commitment.

What matters, of course, is not the **vision** statement in itself, but that every executive and employee is committed to it.

| Hearts and Minds | 'What is a vision? A vision should state what the future of the organisation will be like. It should engage our hearts and our spirits; it is an assertion about what we and our companies want to create. It is something worth going for; it provides meaning to the people in the organisation, in the work they are doing.' |
|---|---|

So said a leading American expert, Warren Bennis.

| Commitment | He says that the questions you should ask before drafting a vision statement are: |
|---|---|

- What is unique about your company?

- What values are true priorities for the next decade?

- What would make me personally commit my mind and heart to this **vision** over the next 10 years?

- What does the world really need that our organisation can and should provide?

- What do I really want my organisation to accomplish that I will be committed, alive and proud with my association with it?

| Outstanding Executives | In a study of 50 outstandingly successful chief executives, Warren Bennis identified the common characteristics they possess. |
|---|---|

- They develop a compelling **vision** of the firm's future.

- They translate the **vision** into reality by concentrating on the key to success.

- They remain deeply involved at the very heart of things, spurring the actions needed to carry out the **vision**.

- They motivate employees to embrace the **vision**.

- They constantly articulate the **vision** so that it permeates all organisation levels and functions, taking the organisation where it has never been before.

## THE MISSIONARY FACTOR

| Making It Worthwhile | Successful companies give their executives and employees a meaning in life. They know how important it is for all of us to lead lives of significance, to feel that we are making a worthwhile contribution to a meaningful objective. |
|---|---|

| | |
|---|---|
| Sense of 'Value' | Successful companies are able to create a sense of 'value' in their products and services and transmit this sense of value to their customers, employees, and the community at large. Surely this is what Marks & Spencer have achieved through their commitment to employees, suppliers, and customers. |

# COMMUNICATION

| | |
|---|---|
| Promotion | This sense of vision is projected with almost missionary-like zeal by the executives of the companies concerned. |
| | When she started, Anita Roddick was prepared to take every opportunity of addressing groups of potential customers and also to seize every chance of talking to journalists. |
| British Airways | Sir Colin Marshall of British Airways does likewise. Every week several BA directors, Sir Colin included, visit staff training courses and other events to talk to people about what the company is trying to do and why. Whenever he flies around the world, Sir Colin leaves the plane at every opportunity to talk to staff on duty. |
| Visiting Depots | Tom Farmer of Kwik-Fit is constantly visiting every one of his depots to talk to staff on duty. |
| Key Task | In short, **communication of your vision is as important as having a vision.** |
| | It is impossible to over-communicate. |

# PUTTING IT INTO PRACTICE

| | |
|---|---|
| Ask People | I once turned down a consultancy assignment. I advised my client to form a small committee of middle managers, and give them time to carry out the assignment for themselves. As consultants, we invariably find a wealth of ideas within the companies we visit. |
| | To practise what we preach we regularly close down our own company for a meeting of every employee. At one meeting, our telephone receptionist was the star performer! |

| | |
|---|---|
| Involve Employees | When Standard Telephone and Cables said they wanted to be the 'best company', they involved their employees by asking them, 'What does it mean to you to be the best company?' The answer came back clearly: |

- to be efficient, profitable, and give good service to our customers.

| | |
|---|---|
| Test Your Vision | Bernard Audley, the Chairman of AGB, says that 'I have to keep testing our vision and constantly updating it'. So, every other year they assemble the top staff from 20 different countries involving 200 key people to monitor, refine, or redefine the vision. |

| | |
|---|---|
| Heartfelt | I was going to say that expressing your **vision** requires you to do some hard thinking. In a sense, it does. You do need to think very hard about the questions Warren Bennis posed on page 38. But, at another level, if you can really 'speak from the heart' in seeking to express the **vision** you are seeking to achieve, it should be relatively easy. |

If you are running a 'one-man business' (or one-woman), find a friend with the intellectual ability and the empathy to help you express your thoughts succinctly.

| | |
|---|---|
| Extrovert Leadership | Let us stop and reflect on some of the words we have been using: |

Vision

Heartfelt

Enthuse

Motivate

Communicate

Missionary Zeal

All these words come back to the earlier comment about successful companies being led by extroverts, while less successful companies are led by introverts.

It requires a great effort to change ourselves into the extrovert approach of an Anita Roddick or Jan Carlzon, but enthusing others in our **vision** is a key aspect of success.

## 2 ASSESS VIABILITY

That you **DEFINE** your market-place by a thorough understanding of all existing or potential customers, their total purchases, and thus the **VIABILITY** of the market share you seek to achieve.

Further, that you **UNDERSTAND** all the direct and indirect influences shaping the future size and **STRUCTURE** of your market-place.

## A REASON FOR FAILURE

A Silly Mistake?

A dress shop in a small town could not cope with three more fashion conscious, **customer-orientated** competitors. So the owner closed down her shop, invested her savings in having it refurnished, and reopened as a shop specialising in wedding dresses.

Had she rung the local Registrar of Marriages she would have found that the total number of marriages in the town were between 75 and 100 a year. Moreover, had she stopped to think about her potential customers, she would have realised that the bride, and the mother, would want to go to the nearby 'county' town to buy matching shoes, and all the other incidental accessories.

Because she failed to assess her customer potential, the refitted shop closed down within six months!

Many businesses, large and small, make the same mistake.

## A REASON FOR SUCCESS

Enhance Profitability

If you can correctly assess the viability of your market-place, you can enhance your profitability.

## FIND MORE PROFITABLE CONTRACTS

Chasing Business

A typical building contractor or sub-contractor is not very customer-orientated. Normally he regards selling as something which has to be done whenever the order book starts to look a bit thin.

Because even the sales activity is not planned, companies of this type often 'chase after' business and end up with contracts scattered far and wide.

41

Given the expense of transferring workers, materials, and equipment, these far-flung contracts tend to lose rather than make money.

**Customer Analysis**

Some 72 per cent of the turnover of Paul Whiting, the surfacing and landscaping subsidiary of the Wilson Group, came from surfacing. Of this 72 per cent, most of the work came from just three local authorities (*Industrial Marketing Digest*).

As a result, the company was very vulnerable to any cutbacks by these authorities, and needed to have a definite plan for gaining profitable business.

**Size of Local Market**

The key question became, was there enough work within, say, a 30-mile radius of their base?

Working partly on the industry's 'rule of thumb' that 5 per cent of all construction expenditure is spent on road surfacing; partly on the relevant density per square mile of roads in and around the West Midlands; and partly on information obtained from the County Council's Engineers Department; it was calculated that the total annual value of surfacing work was £87 million. The Inner West Midlands core of this was estimated to be £17 million for the public authorities and £41 million for the private sector.

**Viable Local Segment**

The significance of these figures was that they showed that there was a viable market-place within the more profitable 30-mile radius of their base.

With this information, the company was able to draw up a plan for a sustained effort to ensure that the company was on all the local authorities' tender lists and to open up new contacts among architects, builders, and other industrial firms likely to require surfacing; particularly as new housing and industrial estates were developed.

# FINDING WORTHWHILE EXPORT MARKETS

**Exporting Generators**

Many developing countries – hit by the world recession – have not had the funds with which to buy generating equipment.

**World Market Intelligence**

A company making generating sets recruited an economist who understood their market. He analysed their market, country by country, more precisely. Opportunities exist in those countries where output is growing faster than the national electricity generating capacity. They also exist where international development agencies and banks have approved development loans. *(Industrial Marketing Digest.)*

Mexico

Thus, investment in Mexico was influenced by the fact that Mexico had oil reserves second only to those of Saudi Arabia; that it was the world's fastest growing oil producer, with America now buying more oil from Mexico than from Saudi Arabia.

Thailand

Thailand was found to be a promising market because of its geography. The country is long, thin and rocky, with lots of small isolated pockets of population: all of which make a power grid system difficult and costly. Hence, plenty of opportunities for generating sets.

# UNNECESSARY DIVERSIFICATION

Struggling for Business

Typically, because a company is struggling for business, it seeks to increase sales by trying to break into other markets.

Threat

One service company with a total turnover of around £1 million was scratching around for additional sources of business because it was serving an industry going through rationalisation.

Opportunity

It applied Step Two. It realised that it was achieving 1 per cent of a £100 million market.

If it doubled its turnover to £2 million, it would still be achieving only 2 per cent of its potential. Moreover, its target customers were those least likely to be affected by any rationalisation.

# WHAT BUSINESS ARE YOU IN?

Defining Your Market-place

You might be perfectly clear about the business you are in. But it might be worthwhile having a quick look at Step Three before you define your market-place.

| | |
|---|---|
| Product-led or Customer-driven | One company, Edgar Vaughan, had been **product-led**. It viewed itself as being in the business of making fluids from mineral oils to help the traditional 'metal-bashing' industries. *(Industrial Marketing Digest.)* |
| | When it became **customer-driven**, it analysed the way in which its **products** benefited customers. It then realised that it was in the business of **aiding and enhancing production** processes. It was no longer limited to the traditional 'metal-bashing' industries. It could serve a range of industries, including high technology aircraft – which needed its particular form of expertise to aid their production. |
| Worthwhile Question | So, when you are looking at your total potential market-place, do so on the basis of the way in which you benefit the customers you are seeking to serve. |

## ESSENTIAL SECOND STEP

But for the need to keep this book of a reasonable length, story after story could be told of companies which succeeded because of the tremendous amount of trouble they took to **understand** their market-place.

## FUNDING YOUR GROWTH

| | |
|---|---|
| Impossible to Stand Still | In practice, no business can stand still. Ever-increasing costs push most companies into growth. To finance this growth, they need to raise money. I know of several companies which were turned down for no other reason than that they had not **assessed** the viability of their existing and potential market. |
| Gaining Finance For Growth | An essential element of presentation to gain financial backing is the ability to answer questions from the bank manager along the lines of: |

- What do you estimate to be the total size of your market-place?

- What market share are you achieving at present?

- What market share do you think you can achieve, and how do you intend to gain this increase in penetration?

So, you need to be in a position to answer these and all related questions whenever you seek finance for growth.

# FINDING THE INFORMATION

No Shortage — There is no shortage of information for most trades and industries.

Department of Trade and Industry — The Department of Trade and Industry, and other appropriate Government departments, publish statistics in a variety of publications.

Trade Associations — Most trades and industries have an appropriate association, most of which publish statistics relating to the activities of member firms and answer queries.

### IRON CASTINGS PRODUCTION BY INDUSTRIAL SECTION

| | Auto-mobile | Ingot moulds | Pressure pipes and fittings | Building and domestic | Engineer-ing | Other | Total (m) |
|---|---|---|---|---|---|---|---|
| | | | thousand tonnes | | | | |
| 1978 | 908.1 | 273.4 | 303.0 | 293.7 | 436.6 | 405.3 | 2.62 |
| 1979 | 914.1 | 269.2 | 302.2 | 293.4 | 402.2 | 399.1 | 2.58 |
| 1980 | 629.3 | 115.6 | 208.9 | 259.2 | 309.8 | 307.4 | 1.83 |
| 1981 | 522.6 | 200.7 | 230.6 | 214.9 | 218.5 | 242.6 | 1.63 |
| 1982 | 445.5 | 163.8 | 273.7 | 234.5 | 177.7 | 194.6 | 1.49 |
| 1983 | 402.0 | 147.5 | 265.8 | 199.0 | 238.2 | 181.7 | 1.43 |
| 1984 | 377.0 | 159.5 | 227.0 | 184.0 | 289.0 | 140.0 | 1.37 |
| 1985 | 227.5 | 102.0 | 161.0 | 221.0 | 312.0 | 138.0 | 1.20 |
| 1986 | 244.0 | 65.0 | 181.0 | 199.0 | 255.0 | 134.0 | 1.07 |

*Source: DTI and British Foundry Association.*

News Media — All organisations seeking your advertising support – TV, radio, newspapers, and magazines – will help you to assess your local, regional, or even national market-place. If you ask, they will often give you comprehensive manuals or reports free!

Local Authorities — Local authorities – particularly those keen to encourage employment – will often have or find out all the facts and statistics you need.

If you go to the local reference library, you will probably find a skilled librarian able to point you in the right direction.

Trade Magazines — Specialist newspapers, like the *Financial Times*, and trade magazines will often publish statistical data relating to a particular trade or industry.

| | |
|---|---|
| Mastering the Information | In fact, the problem is that you will get mental indigestion from being given too much information. |
| Advice | There are many sources of advice. There are students studying marketing who need projects. As part of its campaign to help business, the Department of Employment will provide two days of consultancy if you ring Freefone Enterprise, while the Department of Trade and Industry has recently launched a comprehensive range of advisory services under its Enterprise Initiative schemes. |
| Surveys | If the specific information you need for your business is not generally available, how do you find it? One way is to carry out a survey. |
| | Design a questionnaire and send this to existing and potential customers. Put it to them that you are seeking to meet their needs, so could they help you by telling you what their needs are. |
| | One English company providing French commercial translations wrote such a letter to French industrial companies. This not only helped to test the viability of the market but also gained a significant amount of business in its own right. *(Industrial Marketing Digest.)* |
| Accounts | Every company has to file its accounts. These provide valuable information. Specialist publishers extract, collate, and publish regular reports of the results of companies in various trades and industries, notably Inter-Company Comparisons. |
| | Studying the results your competitors are achieving can give you a sensible idea of what you might reasonably plan to achieve yourself, while helping you to assess the amount of business your competitors are gaining. |
| | You can also write to Companies House to obtain copies of the accounts of your key customers to estimate their potential purchases. |

## COMMERCIAL SOURCES OF INFORMATION

| | |
|---|---|
| Importance of Step Two Assessing Viability | There are a number of commercial organisations, who, for the appropriate fee, can give you valuable information about your existing and potential customers. |
| | One such organisation is Market Location Limited of Leamington Spa. |

| Market Penetration Analysis | By taking your customer list and comparing it with the Market Location business database, MPA can show in which business categories your best potential lies and even where you have a high penetration, there are still more prospects to go for. |
|---|---|
| | The potential prospects can be ranked by probable turnover in each category either with a cash figure or as an index. This is extremely valuable in selecting prospect lists from the main Market Location database and thus targeting your sales and marketing efforts to get the maximum return. |
| Territory Analysis | Don't be misled by the quantity of houses and businesses around you. What matters is the ability and willingness of their inhabitants to buy your product or service. ACORN is another commercial service which indicates the different purchasing potential of differing residential areas, as we will see later. |
| Your Most Important Assets | Your business has only two assets. One is the customers you serve. (The other is the employees who serve them.) It is essential that you give priority to making sure that you have a system for organising and using every relevant item of information about your existing, potential, and lapsed customers. |
| | Space does not permit me to mention all the hardware and software available for this purpose. Nor all the commercial organisations, like Market Location, which will do it on your behalf. |
| | What is important is that you recognise the need to find the most cost-effective manner of making sure that you have the information. |

# STEP TWO: DIRECT AND INDIRECT INFLUENCES ON YOU AND YOUR CUSTOMERS

Essential
Understanding

Successful companies are those which thoroughly understand all the direct and indirect influences upon customers and – as importantly – can anticipate how these influences will change in years ahead.

A Useful
Exercise

It is a useful exercise to get your immediate executives (or it could be a group of friends) to list all the changes which have affected your private life, and your business life, in the past five, 10, and 15 years.

Companies which can do this perceptively can gain a unique competitive advantage for themselves.

Agents of
Change

The agents of change are five:

- legislative and political
- economic
- demographic
- technological
- and cultural.

Changes in all these areas alter customer perceptions and hence – at the very least – the way in which products and services are **positioned**.

## LEGISLATION AND POLITICS

Legislation

You will be aware of the way in which legislation affects your customers and the way in which you run your business.

Some legislation will create business opportunities. For example, Health and Safety Legislation can create a need for Health and Safety services. So, it is worthwhile watching the impact of legislation on your customers.

| | |
|---|---|
| Political Climate | In Britain, and other countries, there has been a trend towards a climate encouraging 'self-help' and the encouragement of small businesses.

There is a more liberal climate, with greater freedom of individual choice which is reflected in the relaxing of 'opening hours' for pubs and probable easing of regulations relating to Sunday shopping. |

# THE ECONOMY

| | |
|---|---|
| Impact on Business | The comparative economic strengths of one country against another influence the relative values of their currencies. As a result, we may have more or less money to spend when we go on holiday; our imports may cost us more if the pound is weak; and our exports will earn less if the pound is stronger! |
| 1992 | The creation of a true open market in Europe in 1992 is one economic change with far reaching implications. |
| Economic Forecasts | The amateur sailor who sets out on a journey without studying the weather forecast would be regarded as foolhardy. As business executives, we need to be well aware of forecasts relating to the climate within which we will be operating our businesses. |
| Henley Centre for Forecasting | Because it is vital to understand the influences which may affect the future of our business, there are commercial organisations that devote themselves to meeting our needs. The Henley Centre for Forecasting is a leading company in this field. Some of its predictions are given below. |
| Consumer Spending | Will be slower than in the mid-eighties but the cumulative effect of increasing affluence will still be great. |
| Unemployment | Will continue to be a problem. Female employment, especially part-time, will rise and thus give women greater spending power. There will be a growing gap between **core workers** and **periphery workers** who will be increasingly part-time, temporary, and outside the company's career structure. |
| Income Inequality | Will continue to grow, with the affluent getting more affluent while the poor get poorer. Henley points out that this will give opportunities at both the premium and the discount end of most markets but pose middle-range brands with difficulties. |

# FACTORS AFFECTING YOUR LOCATION

M25 Ring
M4 Corridor

Economic factors can affect your location. Thus, if you live in the home counties, you will be aware of the impact of the M25! The M4 'corridor' is extended from Slough to Reading and down to Swindon.

South Wales

Similarly, South Wales has enjoyed great success, with major international corporations setting up shop in its valleys and towns, including twelve Japanese companies. Their influx has not only provided the much-needed jobs but has been instrumental in helping the Welsh to develop high technology industries such as the production of television sets, video recorders, and electronic typewriters. At the moment, South Wales is also trying to follow the example of Edinburgh in setting itself up as a centre of financial services.

So, if you happen to be in fields related to semi-conductors or financial services, South Wales could be an important area to prospect.

Local
Developments

Significant changes in our market-place can creep up on us unawares. I once asked a client to do a study of all the industrial estates and science parks in his area. He found quite a few of which he was unaware, because they lay in areas which he had no reason to visit.

Information
Available

Information of this type is normally freely available. Most local and regional authorities publish 'development plans', while 'Development Agencies' will actively assist companies seeking to develop business in their area.

# DEMOGRAPHICS

Measuring
People

Demographics (demos = people + measurement) is a measurement of people.

Crucial Trends

Demographics is the basis of valuable information about future business opportunities. Moreover, key trends are predictable. New workers for the year 2000 are alive today. They will be the old age pensioners of the year 2050!

Shoe Shop    As one practical example, a shoe manufacturer accurately predicted that the 'baby boom' of the 1960s would eventually create a 'teenage boom'. So, it created a new and totally different chain of shoe shops especially for teenagers.

Birth Cycles    As these 'baby boomers' grow up, the number of young adults in the age group 16–24 will decline by 2 million. But, as they start having children of their own, opportunities for baby products and services that cater for the needs of people with young children will increase.

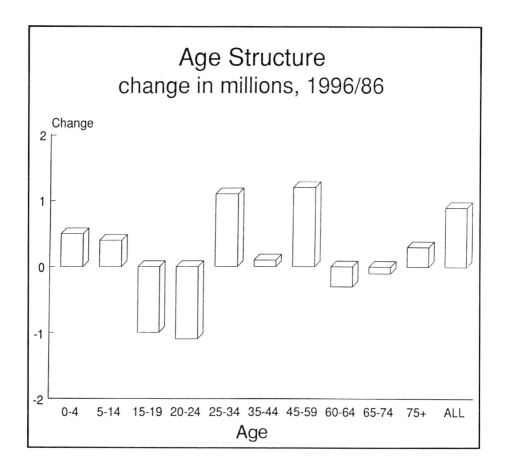

Unmet Needs    The other group that will grow in both numbers and spending power (due partly to the way in which they will inherit the houses and other possessions of their parents) will be the middle-aged (those between the ages of 45 and 59).

These have been called the **GLAMS** (grey, leisured, affluent, and mature) or **WOOPIES** (well off older people).

| | |
|---|---|
| Glams or Woopies | They are among the wealthiest of all spending groups, their financial prosperity being based on five factors: |

- **Property Values.** They bought their first property before the 1970s' boom, so the value of their property has soared beyond belief, while the relative cost of their mortgage has diminished.

- **Inheritance.** They are the generation most likely to inherit property and other assets from their parents.

- **'Empty Nests'.** Their children are now grown up and no longer a financial burden, enabling them to move down to a smaller house.

- **Savings.** They have a higher proportion of savings waiting to be unlocked than any other age group. The over-55s alone account for over two-thirds of all private savings.

- **Occupational Pension.** They are among the first to benefit from the growth of occupational schemes, which gives them a higher level of disposable income.

| | |
|---|---|
| Untapped Market | The research organisation AGB has pointed out that: |

- the over-65s are three times as likely as young consumers to buy food such as canned fruit and twice as likely to buy cream.

- no marketing effort is directed towards the over-55s for luxury durables such as microwave cookers or video cassette recorders.

Other research has shown that older people often collect new products to compensate for their age and to prove that they are still alive and bright.

| | |
|---|---|
| Employment Opportunity | One American bank, Citibank, accurately predicted, from demographic statistics, the growth of young, well educated, and highly ambitious women in the workforce. It saw this fact as an opportunity to fundamentally change the image of Citibank. It set out to recruit a high proportion of these women. This enhanced its ability to recruit high quality staff (on which every business depends) but, as importantly, it helped to create an image that Citibank was interested in, and able to serve, the increasing proportion of 'career women' entering business. In so doing, it gained a competitive advantage. |

| | |
|---|---|
| Older Workers | You must have heard the warning that because of the changing pattern of age groups, there will not be enough young income-earning workers to maintain the pensions of the retired. Certainly, all businesses will need to find a way of using older workers, the retirement age may be ignored and an increasing proportion of customers may also be elderly. |
| Local Demographics | Statistics show the gradual migration of people from the North to the South-East, with obvious implications on the location of the businesses needed to serve them. |
| | They also show the growth of local ethnic communities who have different needs to be met in very specific ways. |

## CHANGING TECHNOLOGY

| | |
|---|---|
| Technology | You will be aware of how the increasing pace of technological change is affecting your own industry or profession. |
| CAD/CAM | To survive in highly competitive international markets, traditional labour-intensive industries have had to turn to capital-intensive systems, including computer-aided design and computer-aided manufacturing. |
| Manufacturing: A Service Function | Mass production, like mass marketing, is out of date. Ricoh (a Japanese manufacturer of computers, photocopiers, and similar equipment) can make copiers in batches of 500. It then alters the details and switches to manufacturing another batch for another market or segment. |
| | The factory of the future will run for 35 minutes on one thing, 20 on another. Manufacturing will become a service function. (This underlines the importance of Steps Four and Five, when we will be discussing the importance of meeting the specific needs of specific groups of customers.) |
| Electronics | Every walk of life has been affected by the growth of electronics and computerisation. |
| | Now we are heading towards 'paper-less communication' where one computer talks to another. Thus, Tom Farmer's Kwik-Fit organisation can – overnight – debit the computers of their customers with the cost of the work done on that day. |

| | |
|---|---|
| Lasers | Once traditional, 'metal-bashing' type work has been replaced by laser engineering. |
| Every Business Affected | You will be able to think of many examples known to you. You will have read of dramatic changes in printing technology affecting Fleet Street newspapers. You will know the impact of changing technology on your own business. |
| | Many of these changes give us greater opportunity to reduce our costs and meet the needs of our customers better. |

## SOCIAL ENVIRONMENT: CULTURAL CLIMATE

| | |
|---|---|
| Your Own Exercise | If you, your colleagues or your friends sit down for an hour, you can chart for yourselves the changing social environment, and cultural climate. These changes present business opportunities, and threats. |
| Henley Centre for Forecasting | I am grateful to Barrie Staniford of the Henley Centre for Forecasting for allowing me to quote from the points he made at one of our client meetings. |
| 'Blip' Culture | The gap between the **educated** and less educated will become more pronounced in future; 10 per cent of people may be incapable of reading a morning paper. |
| | 'We are living in an age where people's concentration span is far less than ever before. They are presented with so much information that the selective process is becoming extremely random.' The impact of **visual** media will continue to grow. Thus, the technique of **positioning** will become even more important in the way in which we advertise, and consciously seek to create the right perceptions. |
| Family Portraits | In 1985, one in seven families with children was headed by a single parent. However, this is expected to level off in the next few years. |
| | As the 'baby boomers' of the 1960s marry, there will be a resulting increase in the number of young children. This will emphasise the shift away from a **youth-orientated culture** towards one which is far more **family-orientated**. |
| Women's Contribution | The number of women in paid employment in Britain has increased steadily. The position of women in families is changing rapidly, as |

they become less dependent on their husband's earnings. Indeed, the working woman is now a force to be reckoned with in consumer markets. Full-time working women alone earned £40 billion last year.

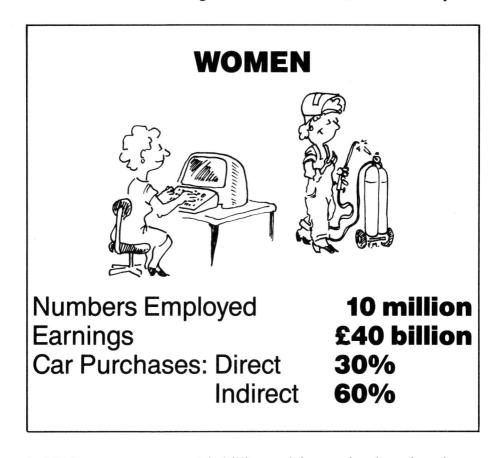

**WOMEN**

| | |
|---|---|
| Numbers Employed | **10 million** |
| Earnings | **£40 billion** |
| Car Purchases: Direct | **30%** |
| Indirect | **60%** |

**Leisure Society**  In 1986, consumers spent £57 billion on leisure-related goods and services. Leisure has become big business.

**Leisure Services**  It is estimated that the growing interest in leisure will create 300,000 more jobs. However, these will need to recognise changing circumstances such as greater family orientation and more interest in physical activities.

**Home-centred**  The home is growing as the focus of our leisure activities. Television/video, reading, hobbies, playing with children, and shopping activities account for 54 hours a week of our free time!

Customers will be focusing on the home in terms of greater comfort and flexibility, better decor and central heating, and increasing growth of telephones, videos, microwaves, and computers.

| Sunday at Hypermarket | Shopping in future will be different. It will take more of people's time. Grocery shopping will be done less frequently – in bulk, out-of-town, and with the car. |
|---|---|

Increase in special interest leisure shopping will be facilitated by the development of a series of out-of-town mega centres with 500,000 square feet of selling space plus leisure facilities and extensive car parking.

**High Street**

Changing locations of shopping will alter the face of many High Streets. They will become more dependent on lunch-time and mid-week business trips. High Streets without a significant office catchment area, facing competition from mega centres, particularly where local authorities have been 'difficult' about car parking, will decline.

**Speciality Centres**

Yet other High Streets will become speciality centres, on the model of Tottenham Court Road (electrical), Charing Cross Road (books), or Savile Row (tailors). Greater affluence, mobility, and leisure will make it viable for, say, Leamington Spa town centre to move towards a regional specialisation in food, Banbury in house furnishings and furniture, Dorking in clothes, and so on.

**Qualitative Changes**

The Body Shop has demonstrated that shoppers are concerned with environmental and social issues. They are concerned with the quality of life.

- In food and groceries manufacturers' brands will have made a comeback.

- **The quality of customer service will be the centre-piece of competition in many sectors of business.**

- New business concepts will develop to accommodate 'life-style needs', a point to which we will return when we discuss Step Four.

- There will be an own-label car!

- More shops will have cafe/bars in them.

- Some pubs will have shops inside them!

**Independence within Families**

Many of the new durables allow us to act as individuals instead of being dependent on the family. Members of the family have their own

TV sets, videos, and may even buy their own brand of food to cook for themselves in the family microwave.

The way in which we present our products and services may need to focus on individual family members, with their own life-styles, and not the traditional 'head-of-household'.

Flood of Information

The increasing flood of information makes it difficult even for 'experts' to keep up to date, and in some ways destabilises society as we are all subjected to an incoherent flood of new ideas or opinions.

Post-literary Society

Henley stresses that we are now living in a post-literary society. One in three Americans may be functionally illiterate and the US Army spends $1,000 per page converting its instruction manuals to cartoons because new recruits cannot read them. The fact is that **colours, symbols, and images are as powerful a force in consumer markets as facts, figures, and words**. The design industry would not be undergoing a boom if it was otherwise.

'There is nothing new in the assertion that a ''picture is worth a thousand words'', but what is new is the increasing influence of a dependence on visual images to convey messages and meanings.'

# ATTRACTING CUSTOMERS

Changing Approaches

Step Eight of our Ten Step Plan is concerned with the way in which we attract customers. The projections of the Henley Centre will have a profound impact on the way in which we attract customers, particularly retail customers.

---

View from Tomorrow: The Service Society

- Successful Containment

- Car Ownership Booms

- Edge-of-Town Multi-Activity Sites

- Liberalization of Hours Restrictions

- Service and Facility Standards Rise

---

| | |
|---|---|
| Growth of Emotion | The 'way we think' is changing from a cognitive or rational process to a subliminal and emotional process. Already many advertisements reflect the trend away from the narration of the 'message' towards an open-ended invitation to 'share the experience'. |

## UNDERSTANDING CUSTOMERS

| | |
|---|---|
| Middle-class World | We live in an increasingly 'middle-class' world. |
| Connoisseur Consumer | An increasing number of people make an occupation of knowing 'what's done' and 'what's not done'.<br><br>If people are making a purchase, they are willing to research and read about your own and competitive products more thoroughly. |
| Health | Increasingly, accepting the disciplines of healthy foods and exercise is seen as an 'investment'. |
| Making Time | Most consumers are concerned with 'making time'. They are prepared to pay more for 'convenience foods' so that the preparation and cooking does not cut into their time. Similarly, they are prepared to spend more for speed of service. Hence the growth of fast-fit service centres and 'convenience' stores. |
| Money a 'Commodity' | Finally, Henley puts forward the view that 'money' is almost becoming a fast moving consumer good, in terms of its provision of the means to not only meet the essentials of life, shelter, and security, but to enjoy a style of life which gives us a personality. Fun has become important. Even increased share ownership has led more people to a recognition that finance can be fun. |
| Life-style Culture | Increasingly, the way in which we need to identify and attract our customers relates to the 'life-styles' of these customers.<br><br>They are healthier, they have made more time, they pack more into their lives, they get more for their money, primarily because they know more. All of which also means they have more (in absolute terms) to spend. |

# STRUCTURE OF INDUSTRY

Impact of
Structure

The structure of your industry will have an impact on levels of profitability.

Harvard Professor Michael Porter is the leading writer in this field. The chart is a modified illustration from one of his books. These factors need to be studied when assessing both the current and future viability of your business.

Competitors

The number of competitors in your industry may have an impact on your profitability, though our experience has been that if you really set out to satisfy customer needs, you will out-perform competitors.

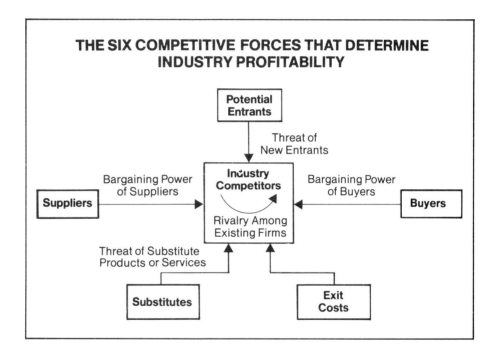

THE SIX COMPETITIVE FORCES THAT DETERMINE INDUSTRY PROFITABILITY

Exit Costs

If there are too many competitors, in theory the unprofitable ones will 'go to the wall'. Some take a long time to 'die', partly because of the stigma of failure, and partly because of redundancy and other costs of closure.

New Entrants

The fact that there may be too many 'conventional' competitors does not prevent new competitors, possibly in a different format. Thus, the conventional garden centre now faces competition from 'Do It All' and similar leisure superstores.

Substitutes
Sometimes your customer may have the option of spending his money in a totally different direction. The family considering replacing their car may decide instead on a Summer holiday, or to buy a new fitted kitchen.

Customers
Your customers may be in a strong bargaining position, for one of three reasons. First, they may be a big organisation in their own right. They may be responsible for a high percentage of sales you are currently achieving. Or a significant number of your competitors could be engaged in 'distress marketing' by discounting, give-aways and other promotions and are thus 'conditioning' your customers to adopt a strong negotiating position.

Suppliers
If your suppliers are in a strong position, they will affect the cost of your purchases; unless you can find alternative sources of supply – one of the reasons for Alan Sugar's success in buying components for his Amstrad machines.

Threat and Opportunity
Every one of these factors is both a threat and an opportunity.

## STRUCTURE CAN CHANGE

King Customer
One of the great achievements of Marks & Spencer was that they felt that since they were in contact with the customer, they should specify the textiles needed by their customers.

| | |
|---|---|
| Orders Refused | At the time, manufacturers made what they liked! They resented a retailer trying to tell them what to do, and initially refused to supply Marks & Spencer. |
| Dominant Influence | Marks & Spencer now have a dominant influence, employing their own teams of researchers and production experts to specify the fabrics they will want and the manner in which they should be made. |
| Transfer of Power | As a result, power has shifted from the manufacturers to the retailers, a trend which may follow in other industries. The logic of producing what the customer wants is inescapable. |

## OPTIMUM SIZE

| | |
|---|---|
| Building Your Business | In my book *Building Your Business* (Pan Books) I discussed the importance of optimum size. |
| Small is Beautiful | Very briefly, small 'owner-driven' companies can be highly profitable because the owner provides a first-class, personal service from the basis of low overheads, providing he prices his product or services to his customers appropriately. |
| Problems of Growth | As the 'owner-driven' company seeks to achieve 'second-stage' growth, it needs to spend quite significant sums of money on recruiting, training, and inducting a competent senior management team, and possibly investing in systems and other resources **before** its levels of sales volume and therefore profitability enable it to pay for the investment. |
| Spreading Cost | Larger companies have a volume of turnover and profitability which enables them to pay extra for an appropriate management structure. |
| Small and Large, Not Medium | Thus, in many trades, industries, and professions, very small and very large units can succeed, but medium sized ones are disappearing. This is true in bookshops and for funeral directors. |
| | In advertising, Saatchi & Saatchi have grown by acquisition. Accounting and legal practices are becoming larger and larger. You will know whether it relates to your own business. |

# STEP TWO: SUMMARY

So, let's summarise what is involved in Step Two.

**Total Market**

First, you have to assess the size of the market-place from published data.

If you need more specific information, you may need to carry out a survey to find out what your customers are spending, what your competitors are selling, or both.

**Viability of Your Share**

You then have to assess the viability of the share of this market which you plan to achieve.

This initial assessment is in the nature of a 'ranging shot', to establish the **level** of business you need for viability.

You still need to carry out Steps Three, Four, and Five before you can firm up the precise level of income you can generate from the specific groups of customers (or segments) you decide to tackle.

**Understanding Your Environment**

As we have seen, you and your business are being affected and will be affected by a host of direct and indirect influences.

Truly successful companies owe much of their success to their skill in understanding how these factors affect their customers and thus the way in which they should seek to attract, satisfy, and retain customers.

**Industry Structure**

Understanding the structure of your industry will enable you to exploit the lessons you can learn from the most profitable performers, particularly in relation to their 'optimum' size of operating unit.

## 3 DISCOVER CUSTOMER NEEDS

That you **DISCOVER** the business you are really in by clarifying the tangible and intangible **BENEFITS** customers need and want, including any unsatisfied wants, having regard to how these needs and wants are likely to change as society develops.

## PRODUCT-LED OR CUSTOMER-DRIVEN

Preoccupation with Product

**Product-led** companies are preoccupied with the product or the service they provide.

Being conscientious, they seek constantly to improve their product with minor technical and other modifications.

Features or Benefits

An engineering company was very proud of the weighing machines it made but it was a typical **product-led** company, focusing on **what** it was producing. It did not stop to think **why customers bought** its machines. *(Industrial Marketing Digest.)*

The shop-owners who bought the weighing machines **did not want to weigh** anything! They wanted to establish the **price** they needed to charge their customers!

So, when a new competitor brought out a **pricing** machine, they very quickly gained a profitable share of the market, to the detriment of their long-established competitor who had to fight to retain profit.

## CUSTOMERS BUY BENEFITS

Customers Buy Benefits

Customers do not buy products for their intrinsic value. They buy them for the benefits they will derive.

You and I do not buy an electric drill for the sake of owning an electric drill. What we buy is a facility for making neat holes with the minimum of effort. We are not interested in the technology which enables the drill manufacturer to provide us with these benefits.

| Why<br>Customers<br>Buy | Indeed, it is important for you to know why your customers buy from you. Volvo's research on this point produced the following result. |
|---|---|

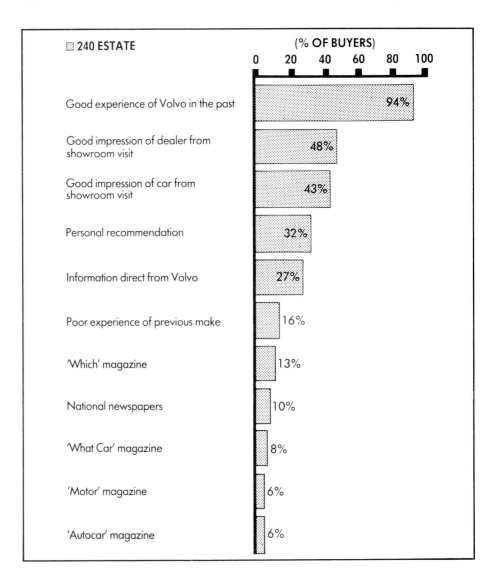

| 240 ESTATE | (% OF BUYERS) |
|---|---|
| | 0 20 40 60 80 100 |
| Good experience of Volvo in the past | 94% |
| Good impression of dealer from showroom visit | 48% |
| Good impression of car from showroom visit | 43% |
| Personal recommendation | 32% |
| Information direct from Volvo | 27% |
| Poor experience of previous make | 16% |
| 'Which' magazine | 13% |
| National newspapers | 10% |
| 'What Car' magazine | 8% |
| 'Motor' magazine | 6% |
| 'Autocar' magazine | 6% |

# EASY PRODUCTION: NOT PRODUCTION OILS

| Edgar Vaughan | Edgar Vaughan's had been a long-established Midlands company which regarded itself as being in the business of supplying metal working oils to the traditional 'metal-bashing' companies in the area. |
|---|---|
| Step Two<br>Factors | It had been adversely affected by many of the factors we discussed in Step Two. The industries that it supplied were in recession. Surviving |

companies were buying less oil. In any event, the new technology of computer-controlled machine tools plus the switch from metal cutting to metal forming were decreasing demand. *(Industrial Marketing Digest.)*

Customer-driven

John Edwards was the catalyst to help his company become **customer-driven**. It analysed the benefits it was providing to its customers. It decided that it was in the business of improving its customers':

- Production efficiency
- General working environment, or
- Imparting an otherwise unattainable characteristic to the customer's finished article.

Partners in Production

The company's slogan became 'Partners in Production'.

As we mentioned on page 44, this analysis helped the company to identify other trades and industries needing its products. We will return to this company when we come to Step Six.

# WHAT BUSINESS ARE YOU IN?

Taking the examples we have mentioned, can you define the business you are in, not in terms of what you **do**, but in terms of the **benefits** you provide to your customers?

# CUSTOMERS WILL PAY FOR BENEFITS

Product-led Prices

One of the problems with being preoccupied with products is that prices tend to be set purely on the cost of production.

A brilliant engineer produces a marvellous new little device, perhaps a valve for the oil industry.

He totally ignores the years he has spent in gaining the knowledge and experience which enabled him to produce the valve. He may undervalue his own unique skills. It costs him, say, £50 to produce the valve. He has read somewhere that a normal cost-related pricing policy is to quadruple costs to earn a 75 per cent gross profit. So, he could decide to sell for £200.

| | |
|---|---|
| Ten Step Approach | What would happen if he applied our Ten Step Approach? |
| | **First Step:** the engineer is a true **visionary**: he does have a **vision** of aiding petrol exploration. |
| | **Second Step:** his market-place is limited to a dozen or so major oil exploration companies. |
| | **Step Three:** under normal conditions each valve may save the oil company hundreds of thousands of dollars. In emergency conditions it may save them millions. They are not buying a valve, they are buying – at the worst – an insurance premium against loss and – at best – they are buying something which enhances productivity. |
| | **Step Seven:** our genius does not content himself with making and selling a valve. He has **created** a total support, advisory, and – if necessary – emergency service. |
| | **Step Nine:** he does not merely sell a product, he really makes sure that his customers are satisfied by the intense level of support they receive. |
| | **Step Ten:** since he is a genius, he is constantly investing his profits in further research to refine and upgrade the quality of both his product and his service. |
| What Business Is He In? | In your view, **what business is he in?** He is in the business of providing a research and advisory service, including, when necessary, an emergency service which aids production and minimises losses. (He is *not* making and selling valves.) |
| How Much Would You Pay? | If you were an oil industry executive, how much would you be willing to pay for such a comprehensive research, advisory, emergency, production-enhancement, loss-containment service? |
| | In fact, the actual valve is only an incidental element of the package. |

## CUSTOMERS BUY BENEFITS

| | |
|---|---|
| Focus on Benefits | You need to focus on the benefits you are supplying or could supply and thus more accurately define **the business you are in**. |
| Adding Value | By seeking to enhance the benefits your customers receive, you are **'adding value'** to your product or service. |

**Benefits, Not Costs**

Customers will pay you a price based on these benefits. You can enhance your own levels of profitability. This is **not** profiteering. These additional profits can be used to invest in better resources to improve and upgrade your services so that you are better able to serve your customers in future.

> Profits are not made by differential cleverness but differential stupidity, says David Ricardo, father of systematic economics.

 **SUB-DIVIDE CUSTOMERS**
That you **SUB-DIVIDE** your market-place by grouping together customers who have any similarities in common with each other.

## MASS MARKETING IS DEAD!

| | |
|---|---|
| Manufacturing a Service Industry | 'Mass manufacturing', where large volumes of identical products were produced to achieve economies of scale, is now coming to an end. |
| | It is being replaced by the flexible manufacturing of shorter runs designed to meet specific customer needs. |
| Mass Marketing is Dead | Equally, 'mass marketing' is dead. Even very large organisations are changing their products subtly to appeal to the specific needs of specific groups of customers. |
| Terminology: Segmentation | Every trade or profession has its own terminology. The technical term for the process of sub-dividing your customers into groups is **segmentation**. If you visualise a grapefruit, you will know it is made up of segments. Similarly, your total market-place is made up of a number of distinct segments or groups. |
| | Let us look at how this is applied in practice. |

## DIFFERENT CUSTOMERS: DIFFERENT OPPORTUNITIES

| | |
|---|---|
| Demographics | The 56 million people who live in Britain can be sub-divided by age, sex, ethnic origin, education, wealth, life-styles, and – in fact – a host of different ways. |
| Profit Opportunity | If you can identify a particular group (or segment) of customers, then you can improve your profit margins by meeting their particular needs in a way which they appreciate. By way of example, let us look at the WOOPIES or GLAMS, that section of the population who are over 55. |

| | |
|---|---|
| Saga Holidays | Saga Holidays established itself in the 1950s as a specialist tour operator for retired people, and its success later encouraged the giant Thomson tour operator to enter this market in the early 1980s with its 'Young at Heart' tour programme. Thomson's accepts that this segment of the travel industry has 'grown rapidly in recent years and is increasingly important for us'. |
| A Unique Tour Company | Saga is not being yet another 'tour company' advertising the fact that it is a tour company in competition with hundreds of other tour companies. It has **identified** a particular group of customers, it is setting out to **attract** customers from this group, it is seeking to **satisfy** them, and it is seeking to **retain** them. All its promotion activities can be more cost-effective, and thus profit margins will improve. |
| Midland Bank | Since older people have accumulated a much higher level of savings than other age groups, they have clearly been a target for financial institutions. |
| | Midland Bank has a special package aimed at the over-55s – called Fifty Five Plus – which includes free financial advice, investment options, and an interest only loan for home improvements and repairs, and special discounts on health insurance and security products. |
| A Unique Banking Service | It is focusing its attention on a particular group of people and, by meeting their needs, providing a service to them at an improved margin of profit to itself. |
| McCarthy and Stone | Estimates suggest that about one in ten of all new private housing is aimed at elderly people. |

An exclusive development of retirement apartments

One leading firm of builders, McCarthy and Stone, plans to build a series of special villages for over-55s throughout the UK. The first, to be built near Oxford, will include specialist leisure facilities such as a golf course, swimming pools, and tennis courts.

A Unique
Building
Company

It is setting out to build houses for the needs of a specific group of customers. Building costs will be lower because it will gain expertise. Its marketing costs will be lower because it will be aiming at a particular type of customer, and thus its profit margins will be higher. It comes back to the theme, and indeed the title, of this book.

Focused
Retailing

These companies, and many more, are practising what is known as 'focused retailing'.

# PRODUCT SECTORS: CUSTOMER SEGMENTS

Product-led
Sales-driven

I was once called in to help a company which made heavy trucks. It had been suffering from the worldwide recession in truck sales. Like many companies, it had long been **product-led**, though the shortage of orders meant that it was now very much **sales-driven**.

Product
Sectors

My approach was to organise a weekend conference of the entire senior management team.

My first question was, 'How do you sub-divide your customers into segments?' The answer was that it produced a 16-ton truck, a 20-ton truck, a 24-ton truck, and a 30-ton truck! This is a typical response of many **product-led** organisations. It was sub-dividing **what it did**. It was focusing on its product sectors.

Customer
Segments

The outcome was that it agreed that it needed to have an emergency campaign to find out which type of customers bought its products and why.

Use of Vehicles

When this information was available, we had another weekend conference and worked out the way of sub-dividing customers. One way of grouping was linked to the type of goods being carried. Thus, they included:

- dangerous fluids

71

- safe fluids
- perishable foods
- minerals and other aggregates
- and so on.

We identified fifteen user groups.

Each group of customers was seeking specific benefits from the use of the firm's trucks.

**90 per cent of Sales**

In fact, we discovered that 90 per cent of all the company's trucks were bought by just four user groups out of 15 (though, as so often happens, it had been dissipating its efforts by going after relatively fringe markets).

**Focus**

So, the main lesson learnt was to **focus** its efforts on four groups of customers buying 90 per cent of its trucks, while carrying out a more thorough investigation of the remaining 11 customer groups to see whether any of these could be turned into major customers, by meeting their specific needs.

# UNDERSTANDING YOUR CUSTOMERS

**Meeting Their Needs**

The more that you, and I, understand about our customers, the better able we are to meet their needs.

One way of doing this is to build up **customer profiles**.

**Who Buys Flats?**

Increasingly, as we have seen already, builders are seeking to build flats and houses for specific groups of potential customers.

Let's consider how many different types of people are likely to consider buying a flat. They could include:

- **Swingers,** young unmarried, active, fun-loving, party-going people.
- **Sophisticates,** more mature than swingers, with more income and education, more desire for comfort and individuality.
- **Newly Married,** focusing on ability to buy a future home, not enough money to buy a house, though two-incomed because wife is working.

72

- **Family,** mature couple with teenage family needing to be near differing schools, colleges, and leisure activities for teenagers.

- **Job-centred,** want to be near job, could be single adults, widows, or divorcees.

- **Home-centred,** former house-owners, probably elderly unable to maintain garden but still want some aspects of surburban life.

- **Urban-centred,** again, former house-owners, whose children have now left home, want to be close to attractions of a city.

| | Distinctive design | Economy | Common facilities | Privacy | Close in location | Room size | Interior variety | Strong management |
|---|---|---|---|---|---|---|---|---|
| Swingers | | | | | | | | |
| Sophisticates | | | | | | | | |
| Newly married | | | | | | | | |
| Family | | | | | | | | |
| Job-centred | | | | | | | | |
| Home-centred | | | | | | | | |
| Urban-centred | | | | | | | | |

**Analysing Their Needs**

How do you set about analysing the different needs of these seven distinct groups of potential customers?

One way is to list the qualities they may need, and then prepare what could be described as a **customer needs analysis grid**.

Perhaps using a pencil you might like to fill in the grid. Put a cross whenever you feel that each of the groups of potential customers would be interested in one or more of the benefits listed across the bottom of the grid.

| Creating Customer Profiles | Very successful organisations devote a great deal of effort to building up these 'customer profiles'. In some instances they carry out their own research; in others they use information collected by industry-wide sources, such as Target Group Index. |

## BURTON'S CUSTOMER PROFILES

| Annual Report | The annual accounts of very successful companies are always well worth reading. Those for the dynamically successful Burton Group are particularly well produced. |

| Step Two: Assess Viability | It clearly applied Step Two when in 1977 it decided, 'to move out of the declining suit business worth £100 million, and into the mainstream of retail clothing worth £1 billion and rising'. |

| Step Five: Target | The way in which it achieved a dramatic success story was to apply Step Five by developing specific chains of shops to meet the needs of precisely defined groups of customers. |

Let us look at some of these specific customer profiles.

The Young Market: Dorothy Perkins    The Style Market: Principles    The Teenage Market: Top Shop/Top Man    The Larger Market: Evans

# The secret of successful retailing is giving the market what it wants.

The Men's Market: Burton    The Knightsbridge Market: Harvey Nichols    The Family Market: Debenhams    The Stock Market

Once again shareholders get something they like the look of from Burton.

Profits up 85% to £148·7 million. Earnings per share up 22%. Dividend up 29·6% to 5·7p. Group sales up 123% to £1·2 billion. Market share up to 9%. Debt reduced from £261 million to £130 million.

They are excellent figures, but hardly surprising when you recall we've returned record profits for the past six years.

It isn't just our shareholders who have profited. Successful employee achievement has been rewarded, and 24,000 of our staff have participated in performance related incentive schemes that paid £13.1 million.

In fact, all of Britain benefited. Our sales of British made goods were up by more than £150 million last year. We created over a thousand new full time jobs, and of the 1300 young people who joined Burton through the Youth Training Scheme, 70% now have permanent jobs with us.

So much for 1986. But what are we doing about the coming years? We've literally laid the foundations, adding 75 new shops in 259,000 square feet of space, including the first new look Debenhams, which opened its doors last month to the delighted families of Preston.

We've invested an all time record £112 million in UK retailing, and since July 1986 created a further 1200 jobs under the YTS. Our community programme continues to develop new areas of activity, stimulating enterprise and encouraging new businesses, particularly in the North East.

If you're in the market for an investment with a future, we're sure we've got the very thing you have in mind.

**The Burton Group plc.**
Successfully Managing Change

**Customers:** men aged between 20 and 40, boys and youths from 5 to 15.

**Fashion profile:** mainstream fashion in a mid-priced range. First Base for 5–10 year olds. Telex for 10–15 year olds.

**Special developments:** the modern, classic suit in hot demand. Largest leather and denim sales in the UK. New formula for store modernisation.

**Customers:** women aged between 18 and 40, girls from 9 to 14.

**Fashion profile:** mainstream fashion in mid-priced range. Perks for 9–14 year olds. Expression for 14 + . Mum's the Word, maternity wear.

**Special developments:** classic ranges enhanced. Widening product range in cosmetics and jewellery. Also leather wear and ski-wear.

**Customers:** girls and fashion-conscious young women aged 9–30.

**Fashion profile:** Top Shop's main ranges are for 15–25-year-old fashion-conscious and trendy young women. These are supplemented by Top Notch, aimed at Top Shop's more sophisticated 20–30-year-old customers, Streetwise for the young individualist and Top Girl, which appeals to the 9–14-year-old girl who wants to look like her fashionable elder sister.

**Customers:** younger men and boys from 10 to 30.

**Fashion profile:** high fashion for the style-conscious 15–25 year olds. Wild Boys for 10–14 year olds. Portfolio, classic co-ordinates, for the 25–30 year old. Physique, leisure sportswear for 18–24 year olds.

**CHAMPION** SPORT  **Customers:** men, women, and children from 15 to 35 + .

**Fashion profile:** fashionable, competitively priced sportswear, ski-wear, and leisure wear for the active and not so active.

**Customers:** aspiring and successful women aged between 25 and 45.

**Fashion profile:** life-style theme – Career Dressing, Daywear, Weekend/Leisurewear, and After Six.

**Special developments:** fashion ranges consolidated and precisely targeted.

PRINCIPLES FOR MEN

**Customers:** aspiring and professional men aged between 25 and 45.

**Fashion profile:** modern classic city wear, sophisticated casual and leisure wear in the medium to higher price range.

**Customers:** women 25–49.

**Fashion profile:** fashion for the fuller figure; ranges Top Lady, Good Looks, The Evans Collection.

**Special developments:** successful introduction of new corporate image.

# CHOSEN CUSTOMERS

Focused Retailing

As you will see, the whole theme of Burton's annual report is serving the specific needs of a clearly defined group of **chosen customers**. I am quite sure that it has a wealth of information about the needs of each of its chosen customer groups.

As a result of this **'focused retailing'**, it had a turnover of £1,339 million in 1987 with pre-tax profits of £240.3 million.

So, understanding the specific needs of specific groups of customers . . . does improve profitability.

# DISREGARD CUSTOMERS

Focus on
Business
Travellers

At a time when most of the world's airlines were struggling for business, and losing money, Jan Carlzon of SAS **deliberately disregarded** tourist and other casual customers to **focus** on the business executive customers. The result, a dramatic increase in both turnover and profitability.

Too often, smaller companies, desperate for business, dissipate efforts by trying to be 'all things to all customers'.

# LEAVING CUSTOMERS BEHIND

By Drift or
Design

It may be that you have drifted into serving one particular group of customers, almost by accident. If you take the time to study all the potential groups of customers you might serve, you may find that you would be able to supply a totally different group of customers more profitably.

Toyota

Toyota has done this. Faced with limitations on the number of cars it can import into Britain, it has decided to import more up-market ranges, even though this means leaving its original customers behind, and moving upwards to new groups (or segments) of the market.

*Toyota Celica GT4 fully turbocharged 4 wheel drive sports car which runs on lead-free fuel, retails at around £21,000.*

| Expanding Companies | Any expanding company may face similar problems. It may have to leave behind the customers it served as a very small company, and seek to move into a different group or segment of customers. |
|---|---|

# HOW DO YOU SELECT YOUR CUSTOMERS?

| Step Two: | You need to know the **total size** of your market-place, and its structure. |
|---|---|
| Step Three: | You need to understand how your product or service **benefits** your customers and thus **define the business you are in** from the customers' perspective. (As we have seen, this may lead you to re-define your market-place! If so, back to Step Two.) |
| Step Four: | You need to understand **every group** (or segment) within your market-place **before** you can decide which group you can satisfy better than your competitors. |
| | So, how do you set about understanding every group of customers in your market-place? |

# DEMOGRAPHICS: THE STUDY OF PEOPLE

| Foundation People | As we have seen already, the basic foundation of all business is . . . people. Demographics is the study of people. We have already seen how some organisations turn this information into sales and profits opportunities. Let us look at a few more. |
|---|---|
| Lifecycle | The lifecycle through which we all progress can be summarised as: |

- children
- teenagers
- young single people
- newly married couples
- married with young children
- married with teenage children
- married without children, 'the empty nest' syndrome

- confirmed bachelors/spinsters
- retired couples
- the 'solitary survivor' – older widows or widowers.

(As we have seen, some of these groupings have now been popularised with names such as YUPPIES, DINKIES, and WOOPIES or GLAMS.)

**Changing Customer Needs**

**Needs** change with age. Thus, in motoring terms, the young may want sports cars; the young family, two-door saloons; the older family, four-door saloons; with the elderly reverting to small two-door saloons.

---

### TYPICAL CUSTOMER PROFILE

# CITROEN

*Most likely to be:—*

*male, around 35 to 44 years old, with an ascending or top management job, probably university background, earning around £15–£20,000, doesn't watch TV because of the time spent on planes travelling and being trendy.*

---

**Purchase Patterns**

Teenagers buy a good many pairs of cheap shoes every year, for fashion, not durability, with limited purses. Older people buy fewer shoes but are willing to pay more for each pair, and are more concerned with comfort and durability.

| Women | Economic independence gives women powerful purchasing power. In Britain, nearly one-third of all cars are sold to women in their own right. More than 40 per cent of mopeds are bought specifically by women. Hotels are recognising the increasing number of professional women by equipping bedrooms specifically for women. |

## The dream cars . . .

THE cars women really WANT to drive are: Mercedes Coupe; Ferrari (any kind); Mazda RX7; VW Golf Cabriolet; Jaguar XJS; GTi (any kind); BMW 635 csi; Aston-Martin convertible; Citroen 2CV; Range Rover.

## And what we buy . . .

SEVENTY-FIVE per cent of new Austin Minis are bought by women, and 43 per cent of ALL one-litre Minis, Metros, Renault 5s, Vauxhall Novas, Nissan Micras, Ford Fiestas and VW Polos.

Moving up to 1.3 litres, women buy 29 per cent of all new Metros, Nissan Sunnys, Ford Escorts and Fiestas, Vauxhall Astras, Peugeot 205s and Renault 5 Turbos.

| Children | Similarly, the purchasing power of children has made many a pop star a millionaire, in addition to those like Richard Branson, who – through his Virgin record shops – sells the records. |

| Abbey National Versus TSB | Whereas the **'customer profile'** of the Abbey National is towards the 21–34 year age groups, the TSB **'customer profile'** is more in the 45 + age group. Indeed, the TSB is endowed with a high proportion of elderly customers and has thus created services specifically geared to this group or segment of customers, with saving plans, life insurance, special annuities, investment, and travel facilities. |

| TSB Research | TSB has carried out a great deal of research to identify what is important to its customers. In addition to caring for the more elderly, it took a great deal of care to gain a thorough understanding of what interested and motivated young people in the 15–19 age group. It discovered that in this age group people value service more than gimmicks and it tailored the **positioning** and **promotion** of its services accordingly. As a result of this careful analysis nearly one-third of all school leavers who opened a cheque account in 1985 did so with the TSB. |

Ethnic Origins We now live in a multi-racial society, which presents business opportunities.

One building society has opened a branch in a predominantly Chinese area which is organised to meet the specific needs of its customers.

# CLUB MEDITERRANEE

**Significance of Statistics**  It is not sufficient just to look at population statistics. It is vital to look behind them to appreciate what they may mean to you and your customers.

The success of Club Mediterranee was not luck. It was the result of very good, creative interpretation of demographic changes.

**Lack of Confidence for Customers**  They recognised that there was a growth in the number of young adults who, while they had more money and were better educated, came from working-class origins. Hence, they might lack the confidence to organise and go on an overseas holiday themselves, which had – hitherto – been a somewhat upper-class activity.

**Customer Benefits**  However, they would willingly join a club which would not only organise their holidays for them, but provide all their leisure facilities at an inclusive price, and – as importantly – provide a club environment in which they could meet those of their own age group and interests.

**Listening to Customers**  In fact, like Richard Gabriel and David Alliance, the founders of Club Mediterranee studied the competition, talked, and listened to young people, so that they thoroughly understood their needs and wants **BEFORE** they built their first resort.

# SOCIO-ECONOMIC GROUPINGS

**A B C D E**  One very common way of breaking down customers is by linking their social backgrounds with their economic status. The groupings are as under:

**A**  Upper middle class, higher managerial, administrative, or professional.

**B**  Middle class, intermediate managerial, administrative, or professional.

**C1**  Lower middle class, supervisory or clerical and junior managerial, administrative, or professional.

**C2**  Skilled working class, skilled manual workers.

**D**  Working class, semi and unskilled workers.

**E**  Those at lowest levels of subsistence, state pensioners, or widows, casual, or low grade workers.

| Launching a Newspaper | You will see these categories used in many forms of customer research. Thus, when the new newspaper *The Independent* was launched, it sent a mail shot to 3 million households. These were aimed at households with 20–45-year-old A, B, and C1 adults, of whom it is estimated there are 6.5 million in Britain.

*The Independent* needed 375,000 customers, representing a 5.7 per cent penetration of its targeted audience. |
| Abbey National | The Abbey National Building Society has a **'customer profile'** which is clearly orientated towards the higher A, B, and C1 groups. |
| Trustee Savings Bank | The Trustee Savings Bank has carried out extensive customer research to identify the needs of its existing customers. These are primarily in the C2, D, and E categories. Though the customers in this group are less wealthy, they are both more numerous and potentially growing faster than the As and Bs who represent the bulk of customers for its competitors. |
| Customer Communications | As we will see later, once you have established your own **'customer profiles'** then everything you do thereafter must be designed to ensure that you **communicate** effectively with your particular customer groups. |

## DANGEROUS ASSUMPTIONS

| Socio-economic Groupings | By 1957, Ford USA had successfully re-established itself as a strong competitor in three of the four main socio-economic markets: the 'lower-middle' with the Mercury, the 'standard' with the Ford nameplate, and the 'upper' with the Continental. The Edsel was designed for the only remaining segment, the 'upper-middle', which was the fastest growing segment of the automobile market. |
| Emergence of 'Life-style' | Ford went to great lengths with its design, based on thorough customer research, yet it was an immediate, total failure. But, instead of blaming irrational customers, Ford decided to investigate. They found that the traditional socio-economic segmentation was being replaced by what we now describe as 'life-style' segmentation. |

# HOUSING AS A BASIS FOR CUSTOMER ANALYSIS

Indicator of
'Life-style'

One indicator of the 'life-style' of our customers is the houses in which they live.

ACORN

One commercial research organisation, CACI, has done a great deal of research to break down customers by the types of houses in which they live. The name of their service is ACORN, and the way in which they group various forms of housing is shown in the illustration.

Probability of
Purchase

What ACORN – and similar systems – provides is an index of the extent to which people in different types of houses are more or less likely to buy your product than those living in other types of housing. Thus, the table below is an extract from a typical set of statistics. This indicates that those living in J34 type housing are 230 per cent more likely to buy a car, while those in J36 are 210 per cent more likely to buy a car.

## A DESCRIPTION OF THE ACORN TYPES

| | | |
|---|---|---|
| J35 | Villages with wealthy older communities | 230% |
| J36 | Detached houses, exclusive suburbs | 210% |
| B6 | New detached houses, young families | 193% |
| A2 | Areas of farms and smallholdings | 191% |
| J34 | Spacious inter-war semis, big gardens | 179% |
| B5 | Modern private housing, older children | 134% |
| A1 | Agricultural villages | 121% |
| B4 | Recent private housing, young families | 120% |
| K37 | Private houses, well-off elderly | 117% |

Customer
Profiles

You can use the ACORN classification to build a 'profile' of your customers. You will need to analyse past invoices, according to ACORN categories and work out the volume of sales you have achieved from each category.

As shown by the following table, it might be that ACORN group B are 45 per cent more likely to buy from you while ACORN group G are 61 per cent less likely to buy from you. Another way of putting this is to say that customers living in B type housing are 4.5 times more likely to buy from you than customers living in G type housing.

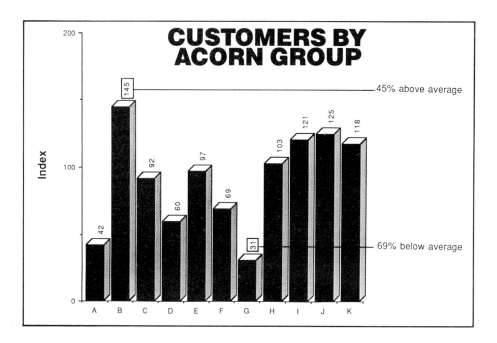

# CUSTOMERS BY ACORN GROUP

Index

200

145 — 45% above average

100

97
92
60
69
42
31 — 69% below average
103
121
125
118

0

A  B  C  D  E  F  G  H  I  J  K

## ACORN Neighbourhood Groups

D Poor Quality Older Terraced Housing

H Multi-Racial Areas

A Agricultural Areas

E Better-Off Council Estates

I High Status Non-Family Areas

B Modern Family Housing, Higher Incomes

F Less Well-Off Council Estates

J Affluent Suburban Housing

C Older Housing of Intermediate Status

G Poorest Council Estates

K Better-Off Retirement Areas

Product
Profiles

If you sell more than one type of product or service, you can see whether the customer profiles are significantly different from product to product. Thus, in the tables below, the profiles of those buying sports cars differ from those buying saloons.

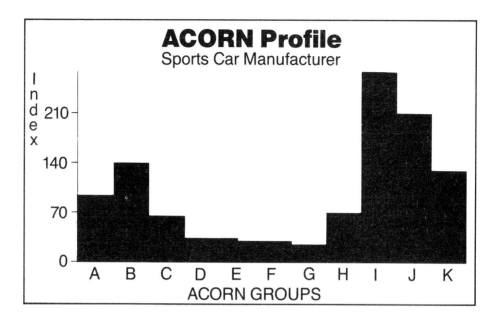

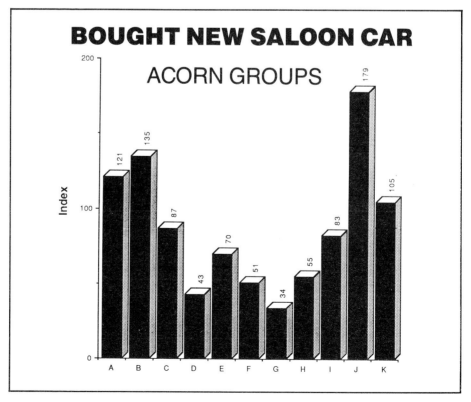

| | Territory Potential | If you sell your product through a network of agents, dealers, or distributors, you may need to assess the potential of each territory. |

Territory
Potential

If you sell your product through a network of agents, dealers, or distributors, you may need to assess the potential of each territory.

If you are planning to open a new business for yourself, you will need to assess the viability of the locations available to you.

Taking one of the earlier tables, if your product is 145 per cent more likely to be bought by customers from B housing and 31 per cent by customers from G housing, the relative proportion of these houses in your territory will affect its potential.

Thus, as shown by the example below, dealer B may have 50,000 more houses, but his sales potential is 500 units below that of dealer A.

## ACTUAL AND POTENTIAL ANALYSIS

| 1981 | Actual households | Potential sales | Actual sales | Sales |
|---|---|---|---|---|
| **Dealer A** | 200,000 | 4,500 | 4,300 | − 200 |
| **Dealer B** | 250,000 | 4,000 | 4,200 | + 200 |

Dealer
Performance

If you are selling goods through more than one outlet or more than one dealer, then you need to have some accurate basis for evaluating each outlet. If dealer A has sold 4,300 units against a potential of 4,500, he is 200 units below target.

But if dealer B sold 4,200 units against a potential of 4,000, he is 200 above potential.

Will Customers
Travel?

An incidental point to this is the extent to which customers are prepared to travel to buy from you. But this again can be plotted: ideally, for each product or service and by each ACORN category. Customers living in B category housing may be so used to car driving that they will travel a significant distance to buy from you. People living in G category housing may be without a car and reliant on public transport.

After-sales
Service

If the product you sell needs subsequent servicing or maintenance, the 'profile' of the customers willing to travel may vary significantly. Customers may be willing to travel to buy your product but be unwilling to travel to use your servicing facilities.

Lancia
Case Study

I am grateful to Ian Norman of Lancia for providing a case study on the way in which he used ACORN very successfully.

## <u>LANCIA – RIFLESHOT DIRECT MAIL</u>

Lancia recognised that national advertising would not provide the most cost-effective communication for its proposed target audience.

Research showed that existing Lancia owners perceived themselves as highly individualistic and that the existing dealer network covered only 60 per cent of the UK population. A national campaign would not only have been wasteful financially but it would have detracted from Lancia's appeal.

It was decided that direct mail, using a database of some 200,000 potential customers compiled from profiles of existing customers, would provide the best communication package.

Based on ACORN demographic data the first mailing introduced the recipient to the nearest Lancia dealer and invited them for a test drive. The reminder mailing which followed in the following month further increased showroom traffic. All mailings were signed and despatched by the local dealer and incentives were offered to those taking the test drive.

Further use was made of direct mail by targeting the women in the household to test drive the Y10 model and in August 1985 as a tactical response to the important new registration period.

Results varied but were satisfactory with a 5.4 per cent response to the first mailing and a 2.5 per cent response from women to the second mailing.

The direct mail target was found to have a high precision having reached a receptive audience, 60 per cent of whom were planning to buy a new car in the near future.

# LIFE-STYLES OF YOUR CUSTOMERS: THE KEY

**Common Sense**  While there is a great deal of value to be derived from a system such as ACORN, common sense suggests that there are still significant variations between people living in the same type of house. One family in a B type house may be highly sophisticated, theatre-going, music-lovers. Their neighbours may be hunting, shooting, and fishing types. Another neighbour may be a sporting fanatic.

**Theatre-goers**  As one example, one of our clients gained a marvellous response when he sent a direct mail letter to a list he had purchased of regular theatre-goers.

Last year, *The Sunday Times* invested heavily in a promotion aimed at music-loving concert-goers.

Increasingly, the way in which you can gain a competitive advantage is to really understand the **life-styles** of the customers you are seeking to serve.

**What Do Customers Do?**  In part, the life-style of your customers will be affected by the type of work that they do. (TV, radio, and newspapers often have detailed analyses of this type.)

Thus, you should be able to find out the split in industry in your area between:

- heavy industry
- light engineering
- office administration
- electronics, computerised technology
- farming/forestry
- educational
- defence
- tourist/holidays
- retirement.

Thinking creatively and perceptively about those involved in these industries, and the companies supplying these industries, may enable you to group your own customers in a way which gives you a competitive advantage.

Needs and Wants

Maslow's hierarchy of needs is a well known statement of human psychology often shown as a pyramid.

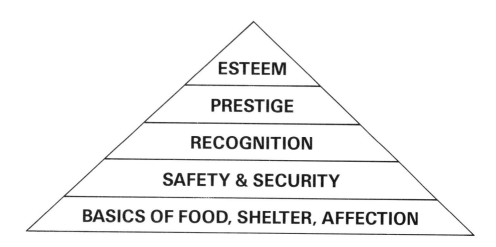

ESTEEM

PRESTIGE

RECOGNITION

SAFETY & SECURITY

BASICS OF FOOD, SHELTER, AFFECTION

## BASIC CUSTOMER NEEDS:
## THOSE WHO SERVE BEST PROFIT MOST

**Survival.** Our first need is for food, shelter, and basic affection.

**Security.** We then seek to make ourselves more secure.

**Recognition.** Having done so, we want to belong.

**Prestige.** As we progress, we want to gain prestige in the eyes of others.

**Self-fulfilment.** Finally, if we are lucky, we want total self-fulfilment.

This basic psychological analysis of human needs obviously affects us both as employers with those we seek to motivate and the customers we seek to serve.

What needs and wants are your products and services meeting?

| Values and Life-styles | A number of ways of trying to analyse consumers have been developed by advertising agencies. Thus VALS (Values and Life-styles) developed by SRI (formerly the Stamford Research Institute) breaks down the nation's adult buying population into eight categories. |
|---|---|

- **Prolongers** (patriotic, stable, sentimental traditionalists who are content with their lives).

- **Achievers** (prosperous, self-assured, middle-aged materialists). The group BMW so successfully targeted.

- **Emulators** (ambitious, young adults trying to break into the system).

- **I-am-me** (impulsive, experimental, narcissistic).

- **Experimental** (people-orientated, inner growth directed).

- **Socially conscious** (mature, successful, mission-orientated people who like causes).

- **Survivors** (the old, poor with little optimism).

- **Sustainers** (resentful of their condition in trying to make ends meet).

VALS seeks to understand the attitudes of those within each category, particularly as regards their behaviour when making a purchase.

| Abbey National | Large companies can carry out their own research. Abbey National invests heavily in researching the needs and attitudes of its customers, competitors, and staff. **Life-style** and operational technology research have given it a deep understanding of its market. |
|---|---|

| British Airways | The successful turnaround of British Airways owes much to extensive research into customer needs, attitudes, and **life-styles** as a basis for arriving at an accurate **segmentation** of the total market-place. |
|---|---|

| Rover Group | I am grateful to the Rover Group and to Systems Market Link for allowing me to reproduce part of the questionnaires they send out as part of a regular campaign to really understand the life-styles of those who buy each model and variant of the cars they sell. |
|---|---|

## AS A NEW OWNER — WE NEED TO KNOW YOUR VIEWS!

Over recent years Austin Rover's success has grown from strength to strength moving ahead with modern technology and the latest techniques. This has resulted in discerning British motorists — such as yourself — driving a range of stylish and superbly engineered models, all designed and superbly built in Britain.

This has only been possible by paying heed to customers' comments and constantly striving to improve and develop the products. This is where your help will be invaluable.

By completing and returning the questionnaire overleaf you will be providing an essential insight into the needs and preferences of todays motorist — views that will help determine our new models and shape the continued success of the only truly British volume car producer.

Please note that no stamp is required, as postage is pre-paid.

**AUSTIN ROVER**

Customer Service, PO Box 156,
Wembley, Middlesex HA0 4XH

---

Your advice, your views are vital in helping us keep in touch with our market.
Because, quite frankly, no-one knows it better than you.
Your help in completing this brief questionnaire would therefore be highly appreciated. The details you provide will be invaluable in ensuring that our products and services continue to meet your needs and offer outstanding value for money.
Simply complete all sections of the questionnaire, fold and seal, and return as directed. Thank you for your co-operation.

---

**1** Please give your name in the way you should be addressed.                                                          AAD 01

1. ☐ Mr   2. ☐ Mrs   3. ☐ Ms   4. ☐ Miss   5. Other Title |_____|

First name |_____|   Initial |__|   Surname |_____|

Address |_____|

|_____|

|_____|

Postcode |_____|

---

**2** Please confirm the details of your new car:
Vehicle Registration Number

|_____|

**Model** *Tick only ONE (1)*

| | | | |
|---|---|---|---|
| 1 ☐ Mini | | 6 ☐ Rover 200 Series |
| 2 ☐ Metro | | 7 ☐ Rover 800 Series |
| 3 ☐ Maestro | | 8 ☐ Rover SD1 |
| 4 ☐ Montego | | 9 ☐ Metro Van |
| 5 ☐ Montego Estate | | 10 ☐ Maestro Van |

**Is this vehicle . . .**
1 ☐ Yours?   OR   2 ☐ A company car?

**3** What were the TWO most important factors influencing your choice of this new vehicle?

| | |
|---|---|
| 1 ☐ Style | 8 ☐ Previous ownership experience |
| 2 ☐ Performance | 9 ☐ Pricing |
| 3 ☐ Reliability | 10 ☐ Dealer special offer |
| 4 ☐ Spaciousness | 11 ☐ After-sales service |
| 5 ☐ Driving enjoyment | 12 ☐ Friend/Relative recommendation |
| 6 ☐ Running costs | |
| 7 ☐ Interior trim | |

**4** What make of vehicle, if any, does this new one replace?

| | |
|---|---|
| 1 ☐ None | 9 ☐ Renault |
| -2 ☐ Austin Rover | 10 ☐ Fiat |
| 3 ☐ Ford | 11 ☐ BMW |
| 4 ☐ Vauxhall/Opel | 12 ☐ Audi |
| 5 ☐ Talbot/Peugeot | 13 ☐ Citroen |
| 6 ☐ Nissan (Datsun) | 14 ☐ East European |
| 7 ☐ Volkswagen | 15 ☐ Other Oriental |
| 8 ☐ Volvo | 16 ☐ Other European |

---

**5** How old is the vehicle which this new one replaced?

| | |
|---|---|
| 1 ☐ Not a replacement | 6 ☐ 4 years old |
| 2 ☐ Less than 1 year old | 7 ☐ 5 years old |
| 3 ☐ 1 year old | 8 ☐ 6 years old |
| 4 ☐ 2 years old | 9 ☐ 7 years old or more |
| 5 ☐ 3 years old | |

**6** Is the person whose name appears above:
1 ☐ Male?   or   2 ☐ Female?

**7** Date of birth of the person named above:
| 1 | 9 | | |
Month   Year

**8** Marital status:

| | |
|---|---|
| 1 ☐ Married | 3 ☐ Divorced/Separated |
| 2 ☐ Widowed | 4 ☐ Single/never married |

**9** Occupation:

| | You | Spouse |
|---|---|---|
| Professional/senior management | 1 ☐ | 1 ☐ |
| Manager in business | 2 ☐ | 2 ☐ |
| Administrator/clerical | 3 ☐ | 3 ☐ |
| Manual | 4 ☐ | 4 ☐ |
| Housewife | 5 ☐ | 5 ☐ |
| Student | 6 ☐ | 6 ☐ |
| Retired | 7 ☐ | 7 ☐ |
| Other | 8 ☐ | 8 ☐ |
| Self-employed/business owner | 9 ☐ | 9 ☐ |

**10** Please indicate the ages of ALL children living at home:

☐ None

| | | | |
|---|---|---|---|
| ☐ Under 1 | ☐ 5 yrs | ☐ 10 yrs | ☐ 15 yrs |
| ☐ 1 yr | ☐ 6 yrs | ☐ 11 yrs | ☐ 16 yrs |
| ☐ 2 yrs | ☐ 7 yrs | ☐ 12 yrs | ☐ 17 yrs |
| ☐ 3 yrs | ☐ 8 yrs | ☐ 13 yrs | ☐ 18 yrs |
| ☐ 4 yrs | ☐ 9 yrs | ☐ 14 yrs | ☐ 19 & over |

---

**11** Which group best describes your annual family income?

| | |
|---|---|
| 1 ☐ Under £5,000 (under £96 p.w.) | 6 ☐ £15,000-17,499 |
| | 7 ☐ £17,500-19,999 |
| 2 ☐ £5,000-7,499 (£96-144 p.w.) | 8 ☐ £20,000-22,499 |
| | 9 ☐ £22,500-24,999 |
| 3 ☐ £7,500-9,999 (£145-192 p.w.) | 10 ☐ £25,000-29,999 |
| | 11 ☐ £30,000-34,999 |
| 4 ☐ £10,000-12,499 | 12 ☐ £35,000 and above |
| 5 ☐ £12,500-14,999 | |

**12** Which of the following do you use regularly?

1 ☐ American Express, Diners Club
2 ☐ Barclaycard, other Visa card, Access, other Master card
3 ☐ Department store, shop, petrol, hotel credit card(s)
4 ☐ Bank cheque guarantee card
5 ☐ Airline club/frequent flyer programme
6 ☐ None of the above

**13** Thinking about your home, do you:

1 ☐ Own, or are buying, a house, flat or maisonette?
2 ☐ Rent a private house, flat or maisonette?
3 ☐ Rent a council house, flat or maisonette?

**14** How long have you been at your present address?

1. I only moved here |_____| months ago, OR
2. I've lived here for |_____| years

**15** What languages, in addition to English, do you speak or read?

| | | |
|---|---|---|
| 1 ☐ None | 3 ☐ German | 5 ☐ Spanish |
| 2 ☐ French | 4 ☐ Italian | 6 ☐ Other |

**NOW PLEASE TURN OVER**

# GAINING THE INFORMATION

**Commercial Database**

The fact that the information is so invaluable has been recognised by commercial organisations who are creating a massive commercial database. Indeed, they will very often subsidise a promotion for the prime purpose of getting those who respond to the promotion to fill in a questionnaire on their life-styles and cultural values.

Having gained this commercial database, these organisations can then make it available for very specific, rifle shot promotions which seek to match the right product to the right customer by using the group(s) of customers with the most appropriate life-styles.

**Commercial Information**

NDL International is one of the companies specialising in life-style research and a montage of some of their case studies is shown below.

**Internal Information**

However, you certainly need to make sure that your systems can, as far as possible, provide the types of analysis of your customers we have just been discussing.

A friend, Douglas Green of Hadley Garages, bought a copy of his Electoral Register for £34 and used this information to plot out his own market territory. Too often, accountants are left to computerise the sales ledger when, in fact, the sales invoicing system needs to be designed to provide you with customer-based information.

**Creating Your Database**

Information on customer groupings may well be available from the sources mentioned on pages 18, 43, and 44. But the only way to gain a competitive advantage is to think more perceptively about these issues than your competitors.

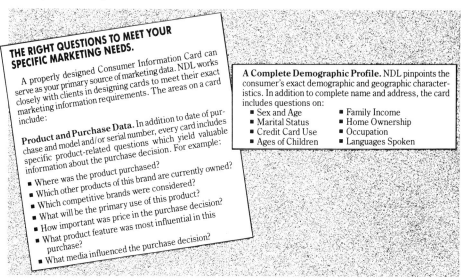

**THE RIGHT QUESTIONS TO MEET YOUR SPECIFIC MARKETING NEEDS.**

A properly designed Consumer Information Card can serve as your primary source of marketing data. NDL works closely with clients in designing cards to meet their exact marketing information requirements. The areas on a card include:

**Product and Purchase Data.** In addition to date of purchase and model and/or serial number, every card includes specific product-related questions which yield valuable information about the purchase decision. For example:

- Where was the product purchased?
- Which other products of this brand are currently owned?
- Which competitive brands were considered?
- What will be the primary use of this product?
- How important was price in the purchase decision?
- What product feature was most influential in this purchase?
- What media influenced the purchase decision?

**A Complete Demographic Profile.** NDL pinpoints the consumer's exact demographic and geographic characteristics. In addition to complete name and address, the card includes questions on:

- Sex and Age
- Marital Status
- Credit Card Use
- Ages of Children
- Family Income
- Home Ownership
- Occupation
- Languages Spoken

## STIMULATE NEW PRODUCT DEVELOPMENT.

A bicycle manufacturer observed in its NDL reports that none of its key product lines was being purchased by a major segment of the young, upwardly-mobile adult market. After further research indicated that certain product attributes would be important to these physically-active prospects, the company designed a rugged, new bicycle that included those attributes. The manufacturer then carefully positioned its advertising and promotion efforts to best reflect the target audience's specific outdoor lifestyles, as identified by the NDL research.

## THE INFORMATION YOU NEED AT A PRICE YOU CAN AFFORD.

The Consumer Analysis Programme delivers extensive first-hand information about your consumers with minimal day-to-day involvement of your company's personnel. Our total control of the operation, from data entry and data processing to report production and consultation, ensures confidentiality to our clients.

Dozens of marketers have found the Consumer Analysis Programme to be a valuable, multi-purpose corporate resource that benefits all aspects of their marketing, advertising and strategic planning programmes. And at a surprisingly low cost.

## HOW WELL DO YOU KNOW YOUR CONSUMERS?

Imagine a scenario in which tens of thousands of your purchasers voluntarily tell you all about themselves. Not only their demographic characteristics, but why they buy your products, what competitive brands they considered, how they spend their time and their money, and what their interests and hobbies are.

Imagine making a consumer database from this information. One that profiles your consumers by lifestyle and demographic variables. That tracks retail sales, determines wanted product features and evaluates retail performance against market potential on a market-by-market basis.

This is Database Marketing from NDL International. We are the specialists in building very large and detailed consumer databases for companies and developing them into powerful tools for marketing and top management decision-making.

## USING DIRECT MAIL TO BOOST IN-STORE TRAFFIC

A major department store chain has built an NDL Marketing Database which profiles the buying habits of its customers. Inactive charge card holders are identified, and direct mail campaigns created which mirror the card holders' lifestyles, linked in to in-store promotions. Each mail-out draws a high response from what would otherwise be 'dead' customers.

## NIKON FOCUSES IN ON NEW MARKET SECTORS

For many years Nikon had a clearly defined target group.

Now, however, many other people are buying Nikon, especially at the consumer end of the market where products like a compact camera with a price tag of under £100 has a mass appeal.

'We need to understand this new market,' says Alan Bartlett, Nikon UK product manager, 'in terms of lifestyle and demographic characteristics, in order to place advertising in the most appropriate media, and to choose effective forms of sponsorship.'

Nikon considered taking on another member of staff to carry out this research but decided NDL was the preferred route.

'NDL,' says Mr Bartlett, 'offered a much more cost-effective and professional option, and they already had a good understanding of the kind of questions we would need to ask.'

How do Nikon feel now, some months on.

'It's a pleasure working with NDL,' enthuses Alan Bartlett.

# SELECT YOUR CUSTOMERS

That you carry out a Strengths, Weaknesses, Opportunities and Threats analysis of your company and its competitors to help you **TARGET** those groups of customers whose similar needs and wants you can satisfy better than your competitors.

## A SUCCESS STORY

One of the outstandingly successful businessmen in Europe is Jan Carlzon who, at one point in his career, took over the airline SAS. At the time, it was losing $20 million a year. The market was stagnant. SAS had already cut costs to the bone to the point where further cuts would have been counter-productive. So Jan Carlzon studied his customers.

**Business Executives**

He decided to concentrate on the business executive segment of the market. He examined every resource, every expense, every procedure and asked, 'Do we need this to serve the frequent business traveller?' If the answer was no, then it was phased out. If the answer was yes, then he was prepared to spend even more money to improve his services to business executives.

At the terminals he provided comfortable lounges with telephone and telex services, gave them separate check-in counters, more comfortable seats, and better food. Business travellers were allowed to board the plane last and descend first.

**Increased Earnings**

In the first year he increased the airline's earnings by nearly $80 million – in a market that was slumping so drastically that other international airlines suffered combined losses of $2 billion. Within three years he had increased the number of full fare-paying passengers by 23 per cent. In 1985 and 1986 SAS's increase in passenger growth continued to exceed over-all market growth.

In a single year he had transformed a troubled airline with morale problems, slipping market share and heavy losses to a profitable business . . . **by focusing on one particular group or segment of customers . . . and meeting their needs.**

# GAINING A COMPETITIVE ADVANTAGE

Your Vision:
Your Mission

Your vision: your mission is to meet the needs of **your chosen customers** better than **your competitors.**

This implies that you **understand thoroughly**:

- your customers
- your competitors, and
- your own company.

Your
Customers?

Before you can **select** the particular group (or segment) of customers you wish to serve, you need to understand the options open to you.

Why should you choose one particular group of potential customers in preference to another?

The answer is you cannot decide unless you understand each group of customers (or segment) thoroughly.

Your
Competitors?

Your decision is bound to be affected by the activities of your competitors. If you have a major competitor who has a dominant share of one group of customers (or segments), then it may be silly to confront him. If as a result that competitor is neglecting another group of customers, then he may have left you an opportunity to meet their needs to gain a competitive advantage.

But, you can't make decisions of this type unless you understand your competitors thoroughly.

Your
Company?

Finally, no company is perfect. It has strengths and it has weaknesses.

It is common sense to try to build on your strengths by choosing one particular group or segment of customers who will relate to, and respect and thus come to require the particular strengths of your own operation.

# UNDERSTANDING EACH CUSTOMER GROUP

**Step Two: Assess Viability**

Having started by studying your total market-place, you now need to go back and study each segment in greater detail.

What volume of business is available from each distinct group or segment of customers, what share can you expect to achieve, and would this provide you with a viable business?

In addition, what factors may have influenced the future of your market? Will the segment grow or decline? If you choose it, will it present opportunities, or are there some hidden threats?

Will it enable you to optimise on your strengths, or put pressure on your weaknesses?

**Babygro Market**

The all-in-one stretch suit for babies did not exist until 20 years ago when an American called Walter Arzt set up a small factory in a village in Fife, hired a staff and started to produce baby clothes in a special stretch fabric which he had patented. In 1986 it went for a full Stock Exchange listing which raised £11.6 million.

Initially, it was in the clothing market for children up to 3 years old, a market estimated to be worth £260 million. According to Government statistics, the birth-rate, which stood at 772,000 last year, will grow by 8.5 per cent to 834,000 in 1992. So, there is a good opportunity for the company.

Babygro wants to expand into the next children's age group, from 3 to 12. This is worth £940 million at the retail level.

**Babygro's Competitors**

Most of its competitors are subsidiaries of very large firms like Courtaulds and William Baird, where children's clothes are less of a mainstream interest.

**Babygro's Strength**

The company claims that its main strength is that it specialises purely in making children's and infants' clothes.

**Step Three: Customer Needs**

Three years ago, Babygro appointed a new Managing Director, Eric Peacock. He has dramatically changed the fortunes of the company. The profits are up from just over £400,000 in 1984–5 and are forecast to exceed £1 million.

One of his actions was to put far more money into **researching his market**. Indeed, it is clear that a great deal of the growth has resulted from a more thorough understanding of the end customer – the parents and their babies – but also a thorough understanding of his own direct customers, which include companies like Marks & Spencer, Mothercare, BHS, Tesco and Boots.

## 'THIRD PARTY' CUSTOMERS

'Advisors'   The sale of some products or services is often influenced by a 'third party'. Thus though a couple may decide to extend their house, their architect will play a key role in recommending which roofing tiles, floor tiles and other fittings they should choose.

Buying       If you sell to a company you may find that you have to negotiate
'Groups'     with a 'buying group' from finance, purchasing, production and marketing departments. In some cases the advice of the 'operator' may be sought.

Specific     So, as we will see later, many companies have to have a specific plan of
Approach     campaign on how they can influence their 'third party' customers.

## SWOT ANALYSIS OF CUSTOMERS BY SEGMENTS

Questions    So, you need to really study each of the customer groups, or segments, you serve, or could serve in a very objective manner. Questions include:

- The current volume of business in the customer group or segment.

- The projected growth of the segment.

- The benefits your direct, and – if relevant – third-party customers are seeking. In other words **'what business are you really in?'**

- The **perceptions** these customers have of the industry in general.

- What **penetration** or percentage share of the segment do you have, or could you have?

- If the segment is growing, what **opportunities** would this pose? If the segment is retracting, what **threats** would this pose?

- The extent to which the **strengths** of your company would enable you to gain a competitive advantage and,

- The extent to which any **weaknesses** within your company would put you under a competitive disadvantage.

---

# SWOT ANALYSIS
**S**trengths
**W**eaknesses
**O**pportunities
**T**hreats     . . . . . .Of each Segment
                . . . . . .Of your Competitors
                . . . . . .Of your Business

---

**Basic Example**  Let's really get down to basics and look at one very common example.

**Tourist Centre Business**  You run a business in a tourist centre. Your 'season' is relatively short. If it is good, it can be very good. If it is bad, it can be horrible. It is dependent on overseas visitors, particularly Americans, who can be fickle or affected by adverse movements in exchange rates.

Do you really set out to achieve a dominant share of this tourist market for your own particular business?

Do you really set out to capture a dominant share of the 'local' customer market which will be available to you 365 days of the year?

Or do you 'fall between two stools' by holding back from the tourist trade for fear of offending 'regulars', but not really looking after the 'regulars' for fear of offending the tourists?

Doubtless, you may have had practical experience of some of these problems if you live in, or visit, tourist areas!

**SWOT Form**  An example of the type of lay-out you might use when carrying out a SWOT analysis follows.

| STEP FIVE: SWOT ANALYSIS OF CUSTOMER GROUP (SEGMENT) |
|---|
| Group/segment ............................................... |
| Current size of segment .................................... |
| Projected size of segment ............................... |
| **BENEFITS** direct and third party customers are seeking. |
| **PERCEPTIONS** customers have of industry in general. |

| STRENGTHS | WEAKNESSES |
|---|---|
| | |
| **OPPORTUNITIES** | **THREATS** |
| | |

## MYTHICAL EXAMPLE: GOVERNMENT SALES

Examples
Difficult

A really professional SWOT analysis is very confidential to the organisation concerned.

So, genuine examples are difficult to show.

However, to help to demonstrate the principle, let's look at a largely mythical example.

Let's imagine that you are an engineering related company, where Government sales are an important segment of your market-place. What might your SWOT analysis throw up?

**S**trengths
- **Reliability.** Proven reliability of units coupled with skills in competitive tendering has earned acceptance in most Government departments.
- **Promotions.** Ability to conduct direct promotions in a specialised, sensitive segment which does not react to consumer-style advertising.
- **Tradition.** Long-established tradition of having done the business.

**W**eaknesses
- **Product range** does not always meet Government requirements and – as noted – forces retention of base-line products.
- **Warehousing.** Have been experiencing management/systems difficulties in warehouses which are still not resolved.
- **Management.** Existing manager is approaching retirement; not developed a successor and have not devoted resources needed to upgrade staff generally.

**O**pportunities
- **Volume** orders can help production schedules and, when relevant, run-out production dates.
- **Spin-off.** Sales of units to Government departments reflect directly on sales to other segments.
- **Image/information.** Dealing with Government departments brings the company into contact with many influential and well informed people, thus providing advance information of significant trends.
- **After Market.** Sales of units in volume pulls through a significant volume of business for servicing and replacement parts.

**T**hreats
- **Reductions** in Government spending – especially in mood of privatisation – could significantly reduce volumes.
- **Price** will always be tight and therefore profit margins marginal.
- **Base Models.** Government inclined to buy basic models whereas strategy is to upgrade models.
- **Competitors** are tackling semi-government/local authority markets as a way of countering dominance in Government sales.

| Question | Could you do a similar analysis for each of your customer segments? |
|---|---|

## UNDERSTANDING COMPETITORS

| Healthy Competition | While the antics of some competitors may be 'a pain', competition is healthy. |
|---|---|

| Customer 'Traffic' | If you are in the book trade, then to open a shop in Charing Cross Road would enable you to benefit from the customers who come to visit your competitors. Likewise, if you are in electronics, the same is true of Tottenham Court Road. |
|---|---|
| | In general terms, where several similar businesses are located together, they benefit from the additional volume of customers visiting the location, part of the attraction of the new mega-centres being developed. |

| A 'Good Competitor' | Harvard professor Michael Porter, in his book *Competitive Advantage*, has a very good section on 'What makes a good competitor?' He defines a good competitor as being: |
|---|---|

> 'One who challenges the firm not to be complacent but is a competitor with which the firm can achieve a stable and profitable industry equilibrium without protracted warfare.'

He adds that diagnosing whether a rival is a good competitor requires the type of analysis we are now discussing.

Finally, he advises that the benefits of having good competitors implies that it may be desirable for you to deliberately refrain from attacking good competitors, but to focus your competitive activities on what he describes as 'bad competitors'.

| 'Good' Market Leader | Michael Porter also comments on what makes a 'good' market leader. He writes, |
|---|---|

> 'If a firm is not in a position to be among the leaders in the industries it serves, its success may well be highly dependent on picking industries with good leaders. The single most important quality of a good leader from a follower's perspective is that the leader has goals and a strategy that provides an umbrella under which the follower can live profitably.

'For example, a leader with a high return-on-investment goal, concern for the "health" of the industry, a strategy built on differentiation, and a disinclination to serve certain segments would provide opportunities to (smaller companies) to earn attractive returns in a relatively stable industry environment.'

His book is a somewhat daunting tome of 536 pages and obviously geared to large companies, but even browsing through the headings and sub-headings can give a worthwhile framework of the concepts he is putting forward.

**Coke and Pepsi**  He claims that, historically, Coca-Cola has been a good market leader by avoiding price competition and acting as the 'elder statesman' of the industry. Pepsi-Cola, Seven-Up, and other companies enjoyed many years of stable profits as 'followers'. In his judgement Pepsi-Cola made a mistake in trying to challenge Coca-Cola, which prompted aggressive retaliation.

**Common Sense**  Because he writes about multi-national companies, it would be wrong to disregard the principles he is putting forward.

You will know of many instances where small or medium-sized companies can create profitable, customer-satisfying businesses by creating a 'niche' for themselves among bigger companies.

The key point to recognise is that success demands that we understand our competitors thoroughly. The questions that we need to ask are related to our own Ten Step Plan.

**Step One: Vision**  Which of our competitors have a true sense of **vision**?

Can we secure a competitive advantage by being **customer-orientated** if they are product-led or sales-driven?

**Step Two: Viability**  Do we know how much business is being generated by each of our competitors? What percentage share of our total market are they gaining?

What is the size and structure of our principal competitors and does this indicate any trends of which we should be aware?

| | |
|---|---|
| Step Three:<br>Meeting<br>Customer<br>Needs | How much work have your competitors devoted to really discovering customer needs and wants? Have they been 'written up' in the trade magazines or local newspapers? |
| Step Four:<br>Sub-dividing<br>Customers | Have your competitors sub-divided your market-place into specific groups of customers, or segments, and which specific segments are they tackling? |
| Step Five:<br>SWOT<br>Analysis | What are the strengths and weaknesses of your main competitors? Have they created specific opportunities for themselves or do you consider that they are facing threats due to the way in which they do business?<br><br>It is important to understand the strengths and weaknesses of our competitors. |
| Step Six:<br>Mission and<br>Culture | Have any of your competitors publicised their own **'mission statement'**? If so, what can you learn from it? If not, what would you imagine that their **mission** is?<br><br>Taking each competitor in turn, what **culture** have they created in terms of their relationships with customers, suppliers, and employees? Is it a culture that gains widespread respect and affection, or one which creates cynicism? |
| Step Seven:<br>Product or<br>Service | How have each of your competitors set about creating their product or service to meet the needs of their customers? Is the actual product or service itself well designed?<br><br>Have any of your competitors 'bundled' their range of products and services together in one integrated 'product'? Or have any of your competitors specialised in providing just one aspect of a product or service needed by your customers?<br><br>What is their pricing strategy?<br><br>How are they **organised** and what **channels** do they use to distribute their product or service to their customers?<br><br>What **systems** do they employ within their own operation and in customer-facing communications? |

| | |
|---|---|
| **Step Eight:**<br>**Attracting** | Taking each of your principal competitors in turn:<br><br>• How do they **position** themselves?<br><br>• What **perceptions** are they seeking to create?<br><br>• How are they, in fact, **perceived** by their customers?<br><br>• How do they **promote** themselves? Have you collected a representative sample of adverts, brochures, direct mail letters, and other examples of their promotional activities? |
| **Step Nine:**<br>**Satisfying** | Taking each competitor in turn, how well do they **satisfy** their customers?<br><br>Have you 'mystery shopped' them? Or carried out any form of research into the way in which they are rated in your market-place? |
| **Step Ten:**<br>**Retain** | Again, taking each competitor in turn, how successful are they in retaining their customers?<br><br>How much effort are they devoting to constantly upgrading their facilities, their systems, their staff training and their other customer-facing activities? |
| **Bash-on**<br>**Regardless?** | Let's be honest, it is possible to 'bash-on regardless' and grow a business; particularly when we are running a relatively small business. But, as we grow, it can be extremely foolish to ignore the competition. In *Moments of Truth* Jan Carlzon writes of: |
| **Overtaken by**<br>**Events** | 'A Swedish manufacturer of welding equipment had long monopolised the European market with its high-quality products. Suddenly the company discovered that it had lost nearly half of its market. Apparently a European competitor was selling less sophisticated equipment for half the price and satisfying both the customer's needs and budgets. The Swedish company by setting its own product-orientated agenda had priced itself right out of the market . . .'<br><br>Whatever business we are in, we must study how our existing or potential customers are having their needs and wants satisfied. |

# UNDERSTANDING YOUR COMPANY

'Know Thyself'

Throughout the ages famous philosophers have stressed that the way to health, happiness, and wealth, is to 'know thyself'. Many of us find this difficult. What is difficult for an individual is often even more difficult for a corporation. Moreover, every strength can – taken to an extreme – become a weakness.

Objective Viewpoint

Many advertising agencies face problems with new clients. The client will brief the agency by explaining how his, or her, company is perceived in its market-place. When the agency investigates, it often finds the client is labouring under a gross misconception.

Perception Analysis

While it may be painful, it is vital that you and I have an accurate appreciation of how we are perceived in our market-place.

It may be that we need to commission independent research to carry out what is known as a 'perception' study.

At our suggestion one of our clients enrolled all his staff in going out into the streets and car parks of his town with a simple questionnaire. What he thought he was well known for, he was not. What he thought he was less well known for, he was!

Yet this man – like so many others – was spending several hundred thousand pounds a year of advertising money on this misconception.

Ten Step Plan

As you work or rework your way around your Ten Step Plan, we need to test what we are doing against two 'touchstones'.

How will what we are doing be perceived by our customers? Will it really meet their needs, their wants, and their expectations?

How will what we are doing compare with our competitors? Will it complement the activities of 'good' competitors? Will it enable us to gain a competitive advantage against our 'bad' competitors?

Strengths

Above all, we need to arrive at an objective assessment of our true strengths in the market-place. It could be that we are particularly strong in the **people** we recruit and motivate, or the **systems** we have devised, or in the **position** we have created for ourselves.

Above all, we need to make sure that we build on these strengths. Moreover, like true extroverts, we need to promote these strengths confidently to ourselves, to our colleagues and – above all – to our customers.

Weaknesses

I was very taken by one point in *In Search of Excellence* which advised that we should 'find someone doing something right'. Indeed, we turned it into a desk display for our clients.

There is a balance between having a 'creative dissatisfaction' with what we do as we search for excellence and a preoccupation with what is wrong. That will give us ulcers, demotivate those we employ, and fail to impress our customers.

## SELECTING YOUR CUSTOMERS

So, selecting a particular group (or segment) of customers whose needs you can meet better than your competitors depends on:

- a thorough understanding of your customers
- a thorough understanding of your competitors and, above all,
- a thorough understanding of your own strengths and weaknesses.

**Achieving Your Vision**

Let us summarise the first five steps we have been discussing.

First: you have your **vision** of satisfying customers profitably.

Second: you have studied the **total size** of your market-place and the factors which may present threats or opportunities.

Third: you have looked at the market-place in terms of the **benefits** customers are seeking (and are willing to pay for).

Fourth: you have sub-divided the total market-place into **groups** of customers, or customer segments.

Fifth: you have devoted a great deal of time, effort, and skill in seeking to **select** one or more groups of customers whose needs you can meet better than your competitors.

Now you need to set out a **mission statement** in which you describe how you are going to achieve your **vision** of making sure that you do **satisfy** your customers . . . **profitably**.

## THE BODY SHOP

**Success Story**

The Body Shop success story is now well known. What began in 1976 as a small shop in a Brighton alleyway, financed by a loan of £4,000, is now a world-wide network of 250 shops in over 25 countries with over 80 outlets in the UK operated primarily on a franchising system.

**Financial Growth**

Growth, in financial terms, has been phenomenal. Starting from scratch in 1976, the firm had achieved profits of £31,000 by 1981. Thereafter they rocketed to just under £6 million by 1987.

| | |
|---|---|
| **Foundation of Success** | There is no doubt that this dramatic success story has been achieved because of Anita Roddick's: |

- **VISION,** which was translated into
- a **MISSION,** which – in turn – has been achieved through the
- **CULTURE** which Anita and her team built for their organisation.

Step One of our Success Strategy was to have a **vision**. Anita Roddick's was to establish:

- **the most honest cosmetic company around.**

| | |
|---|---|
| **Mission** | Since she so obviously 'lived' her mission, let her put it in her own words: |

- **'We produce products that cleanse, polish and protect the skin and hair. How we produce them and how we market them is what is interesting about us. We are innovative in our formulations; we are passionate about environmental and social issues; we care about retailing. The image, goals and values of our Company are as important as our products.'**

| | |
|---|---|
| **Passion** | It is a challenge for me and for you to enthuse about what we do in the same passionate manner. Let us re-examine that last sentence: |

'The **image, goals** and **values** of our Company are as important as our products.'

| | |
|---|---|
| **Image, Goals, and Values** | How many business executives would make this statement? Certainly not those preoccupied with **what** they do. But, if we are concerned with **why** we are providing our product or service, they become more important. They touch upon the all-important **culture** we create to ensure the success of our endeavours. Again, let us allow Anita Roddick to express her own views on **culture**: |

| | |
|---|---|
| **Culture** | 'We will continue to work on the "feminine principles" by "putting our love where our labour is" (Emerson), by being intuitive, and ignoring the aggressiveness of today's business philosophy . . . we will do all this and still open 1,000 shops, still produce new products and retail concepts that will leave the High Street reeling. We will carry all this through with a sense of **enthusiasm, joy, magic and theatre**, which have always been our essential qualities . . .' |

| | |
|---|---|
| **Enthusiasm, Joy, Magic, and Theatre** | Look at the words highlighted in bold type: 'enthusiasm, joy, magic, theatre'. These words are not normally found in books of business principles, though – as Anita Roddick has proved – they express what I believe to be the essential foundation stones of business success: |

- Vision
- Mission
- Culture.

| | |
|---|---|
| **Expressing Philosophy** | Anita Roddick has a booklet in which she dramatically expresses the personality and philosophy of her company. To give a flavour of this marvellous little publication, we reproduce a montage of extracts. |

---

**'Body Shop's** unique ideas, and its caring attitude towards its customers and the living environment make it an **exciting** company to work for."

### EDUCATION

The spirit of education flows throughout The Body Shop. It is reflected in the choices and information we offer our customers; in the training and development of our staff; in our belief in the excitement of retailing; and in the continuing process of discovery and innovation that is an essential part of the The Body Shop. *Susan Jackson, The Body Shop Educational Consultant Writer*

And as Anita Roddick said:

"We will continue to work on the 'feminine principles' by 'putting our love where our labour is' (Emerson), by being intuitive, and ignoring the aggressiveness of today's business philosophy... We will do all this and still open up 1,000 shops, still produce new products and retail concepts that will leave the High Street reeling. We will carry all this through with a sense of enthusiasm, joy, magic and theatre, which have always been our essential qualities ................ It is now time for those who are going to count in the future to stand up and be counted."

### THE ENVIRONMENT: OUR COMMUNITY

The Body Shop takes a holistic view of the world we live and work in. For example, saving the whale and protecting the world's woodlands must go hand-in-hand with the prevention of waste and help for the inner cities, if a healthy symbiosis between man and his environment is to be attained. *Nicola Lyon, Head of The Body Shop Environmental Projects Department*

'Anyone who hasn't heard of <u>Aloe Vera</u> must still be living in space, and any "natural" cosmetics company which hasn't included it in its repertoire ought to be taken to task..' *Anita Roddick*

*"Working for The Body Shop combines for me the supposed irreconcilables of working for good people, and the pursuit of profit, while contributing to the community and environment and having fun! It's also very straightforward as only the BEST will do."*

Peter Tyson UK Franchise Manager

# MARKS & SPENCER: THE ACHIEVEMENT OF VISION

Vision

In Step One we expressed the **vision** of Marks & Spencer as being:

- **'To make a profit and serve the community.'**

Foundation of Success

Though Marks & Spencer was established in 1884, the growth of the organisation as we know it today began in the mid-1920s. Michael Marks' son Simon made a number of visits to study retailing methods in America and returned with the **vision** of transforming his own business into a chain of what he was later to call 'superstores'.

Mission Statement

Any statement which sets out how a company intends to achieve its **vision** we would now call a **mission statement**. When Simon Marks and his brother-in-law wrote down how they intended to achieve their **vision**, they called it 'six principles of business philosophy'. It is a tribute to their perception that the six principles that they put forward in the 1920s are so little changed in the 1980s.

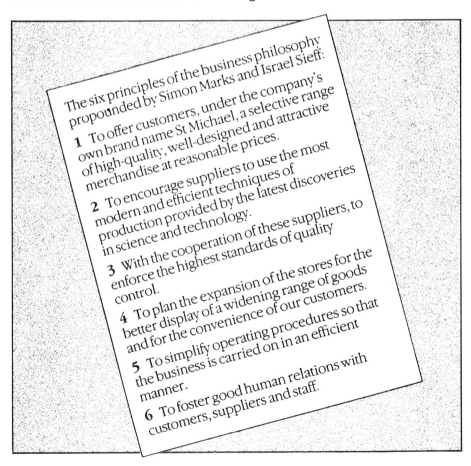

The six principles of the business philosophy propounded by Simon Marks and Israel Sieff:

1 To offer customers, under the company's own brand name St Michael, a selective range of high-quality, well-designed and attractive merchandise at reasonable prices.

2 To encourage suppliers to use the most modern and efficient techniques of production provided by the latest discoveries in science and technology.

3 With the cooperation of these suppliers, to enforce the highest standards of quality control.

4 To plan the expansion of the stores for the better display of a widening range of goods and for the convenience of our customers.

5 To simplify operating procedures so that the business is carried on in an efficient manner.

6 To foster good human relations with customers, suppliers and staff.

## A FEW FIGURES

*Group Turnover (excluding Sales Tax)*

|  | 1985/86 |
|---|---|
| United Kingdom | £3,395m |
| Europe | £94m |
| Canada | £182m |
| Direct Export Sales | £45m |
| Financial Activities | £19m |
| **Total** | **£3,735m** |

**St Michael**

*Five year record*

| Year ended 31 March | 1982 | 1983 | 1984 | 1985 | 1986 |
|---|---|---|---|---|---|
| Sales £m | 2,205 | 2,510 | 2,863 | 3,208 | 3,735 |
| Pretax Profit £m | 222 | 239 | 279 | 304 | 366 |

## INVESTMENT IN PROGRESS

# Marks & Spencer Facts Card 1986/87

## A FEW FACTS...

Marks and Spencer is Britain's largest retailer and sells only one brand . . . St Michael.

Some 90% of St Michael clothing is made in Britain.

The Company buys approximately 20% of all UK clothing production.

Our customers spend £1 in every £6.25 spent on clothing in the UK.

St Michael foods represent some 40% of the Company's UK turnover.

Over 950 manufacturers supply St Michael goods.

Marks and Spencer has 269 outlets in the UK, 9 in Europe and controls over 200 stores in Canada.

Every week 14 million customers shop at M and S.

There are 56,000 staff, 28,000 having worked with the Company for more than 5 years.

Last year, £357 million was spent on staff salaries, benefits and profit sharing in the UK.

## COMPANY PRINCIPLES

To provide clothing for the family, fashion for the home and a range of fine foods; all representing a high standard of quality and value.

To display our merchandise attractively and to make shopping pleasant and easy for our customers.

To provide friendly, helpful service from well-trained, knowledgeable and efficient staff.

To foster good human relations with our customers, staff and suppliers; and in the communities in which we are located.

To encourage our suppliers to use the most modern and efficient production techniques, and to develop a mutually beneficial long term relationship.

To support British industry, buying abroad only when new ideas, technology, quality and value are not available in the UK.

To provide our staff with good conditions of employment and to ensure that they share in the success of the company.

To seek to improve quality standards in all areas of our operations.

## ...A FEW MORE FACTS

Marks and Spencer is one of the top UK companies by market capitalisation, with some 257,000 shareholders.

The Chargecard was carried by 1.2 million customers 12 months after its launch.

Marks and Spencer is Britain's largest clothing exporter, selling to over 30 countries.

Marble Arch store is listed in The Guinness Book of Records as "the department store with the fastest-moving stock in the world".

Some 170,000 people are engaged in the production, distribution and sale of St Michael goods.

The Company is a major contributor to charities and is particularly active in helping to solve the problem of youth unemployment. £3 million of UK pretax profits was contributed to community and charitable activities in 1985/86.

**St Michael**

## THE FUTURE

Increasingly wide, different and exciting ranges will become available.

Over the next four years, Marks and Spencer will invest about £1,500 million on the biggest store development and modernisation programme in the Company's history.

Plans include edge-of-town stores such as Edinburgh, Cheshunt and Metro Centre, Tyneside, as well as satellites for our high street stores.

By 1988 all stores will be equipped with the most modern point of sale equipment, resulting in improved stock availability for customers.

Produced by
Marketing Services, Marks & Spencer, Baker St, London W1A 1DN.

# CULTURE

These principles or **mission statement** not only set out the way in which the company would achieve its **vision** but also lay out the **culture** by which it would be achieved.

Generating
Goodwill

In the M & S philosophy, retailing is conceived as a business designed to meet the needs of the **individual** whether as a **customer** in the store or an **employee** on its staff, or in the employment of its **suppliers**. In practising this approach, the company earns a very large reward in the goodwill shown to it by the public.

Perception

This almost personal relationship of goodwill between the company and its **customers** is based on the **perception** of a deliberate search for high standards of human relationships. So, millions of customers have had a genuine **perception** (a word we will come back to in Step Eight) that in buying at M & S they were, and are, getting better value for their money than they could obtain elsewhere: together with a feeling that in some ways M & S performs a public service as well as conducting a business for profit.

## MISSION-LED CUSTOMER-ORIENTATION

Lessons into
Practice

Any successful company is worth studying, and when it owes its success to a sense of vision, a purposeful mission and a creation of a culture which makes that success possible, then we all ought to put these lessons into practice.

Nuts and Bolts
Example

But to try to put this concept of a **mission statement** into a more practical example, let's go back to Edgar Vaughan, mentioned on pages 44 and 65.

'**Mission
Redefined**'

John Edwards' family had been involved with the company for three generations. He had had the advantage of going to university and then to America to gain a Masters degree, so when he went back into the family firm he was able to do so, as he says himself, 'like a newcomer to the organisation who was unblinkered by the traditional business perceptions of the company'. He accepts that it would be very difficult for any organisation to make the major changes in direction executed at Edgar Vaughan without the assistance of somebody like himself as a new executive, or as a consultant. What John Edwards was able to do was to 'redefine the **mission** of his company'.

## Edgar Vaughan's mission statement

To market consumable products, generally fluids, as part of an overall service package to specific industries. These products will normally improve the user's production efficiency or general working environment, or alternatively impart an otherwise unobtainable characteristic to his finished article.

The products will be sold through a field sales operation which will be built upon a knowledge of that user's manufacturing process or finished product, and that knowledge will be an essential part of the marketing mix applied.

Ideally, the product will be produced in existing or similar manufacturing plant to that used at present, draw on similar raw material sources, and fit into the existing distribution network. However, these aspects are not considered as critical as the marketing approach.

117

| | |
|---|---|
| Important Foundation | Let me quote his own words:<br><br>**'The mission statement which we evolved is now such an important foundation that it is even reflected in our advertising.'** |
| Sharp End Exercise | Let me allow John Edwards to continue to make the point for me:<br><br>'I can state, quite categorically, that though many practical businessmen might regard the effort of preparing a **mission statement** as "academic" we found that the work was truly involved in the "sharp end" of our business. Redefining our **mission** was primarily responsible for ensuring that we, unlike many in traditional metal-bashing industries, did not suffer the effects of the recession. Indeed, preparing our **mission statement** was the "launching pad" of the transformation of our business into one which is expanding rapidly into new fields but which still builds on our traditional strengths.' |
| **Why**, not **What** | The important thing that redefining its **mission statement** did for Edgar Vaughan was that it changed the firm thinking about **what** it did – blending lubricants – into thinking about **why** it did it. |
| End Benefit to Customers | 'Rather than considering that we sell oils or chemicals, we now recognise that we sell the means of **improving** manufacturing processes. The deliberate recognition of the **end benefit to our customers**, rather than the technical processes with which we were involved, enabled our company to make significant changes; in our product profile, the markets we serve, and the way in which we **position** our company and its products in these markets.' |
| Finding a Way Out | When a company is tied to a declining market, it is often difficult to see the way out. The traditional response is to step up selling methods to gain a bigger share from a smaller market. However, this often means that valuable resources are being expended in a largely futile cause. The resources would be far better invested in seeking to understand the nature of the benefits you are supplying to your customers and – from this understanding – to invest in new markets with real growth potential, which enables you to utilise existing capabilities. |

| | |
|---|---|
| Achieving Customer Orientation | The work which John Edwards did with Edgar Vaughan is a classic example of changing a product-dominated company into a customer-led company and, as he emphasises, the focus for this was the tremendous amount of work which he, and his colleagues, put into preparing their **'mission statement'**. |
| Result: Success | Though John has now left, Edgar Vaughan is a very successful company, with both oil- and water-based chemicals which help to improve the 'product performance' in markets as diverse as paper, paints, special steels, aerospace, off-shore oil, and other manufacturing industries. |

## PREPARING *YOUR* MISSION STATEMENT

| | |
|---|---|
| Vision and Mission | Step One of our Success Strategy is to state your **vision**. |
| | Your **mission statement** should describe how you intend to do this. The reason why this is Step Six is that you cannot write your mission statement until you have thought very hard about your market-place, its customers, and your competitors by carrying out Steps Two, Three, Four, and Five. |
| Step Two: Assess | First, you need to assess your market-place. At the same time, you must understand thoroughly all the direct and indirect influences shaping its future size. |
| | Edgar Vaughan's was facing a market decline in business for two reasons. Its traditional 'metal-bashing' customers were in decline but also new computer-aided design, laser cutting, and other techniques were totally changing the technology being used. |
| Step Three: Benefits to Customers | Since your mission statement should start with the **benefits** you intend to provide to your customers, you need to discover how your customers perceive the benefits they derive from the product or service you supply. |
| | It's not **what** you do, it's **why** your customers buy it that counts. |
| | Edgar Vaughan used to regard itself as selling oils or chemicals. Having carried out Step Three, it realised that it sold a means of improving manufacturing processes. |
| | What benefits do your customers derive from buying your product or service from you? |

Did you notice the byline in the Edgar Vaughan advertisement? 'Let us become your **Partners in Production**'. What a lovely way of describing the firm.

I bet that it could not have thought of that byline until after it had really thought through the benefits it was providing to its customers.

As a result, it was able to redefine its market-place, and it could go back to Step Two to measure the sizes of the additional markets open to it.

|  |  |
|---|---|
| Step Four: Customers | As we agreed earlier, you need to sub-divide your market-place by grouping together customers who have similarities. |

You then need to find out the relative size of each group of customers or market segment. If you remember, Babygro found that the market for children under 3 was worth £260 million, whereas the market for children between 3 and 12 was worth £940 million.

|  |  |
|---|---|
| Step Five: Target | Finally, in Step Five we need to carry out an analysis of the strengths and weaknesses of our competitors, and our company. In this way, we can build on our own strengths and opportunities and **target** relevant groups of customers whose similar needs and wants we can satisfy better than our competitors. |

If you refer back to the Edgar Vaughan mission statement, you will see that it regards its strength as being the fact that it has a very strong field sales operation where the salesmen have an in-depth knowledge of the customer's manufacturing processes.

In other words, if it is truly going to be 'Partners in Production', it will not merely sell the products but it will make sure that it does so by providing all the relevant supporting information and advice.

In this way, its **mission statement** commits it to the **organisational structure** it needs to achieve its **mission**.

## PREPARING YOUR OWN MISSION STATEMENT

Having carried out Steps Two, Three, Four, and Five, you can now define your own **MISSION**.

Different companies do this in different ways, but the main elements are:

- The customers you intend to serve.
- The way in which you will meet their specific needs.

- The culture you will create.
- Your profit objective.


# MONTAGE OF MISSIONS

Learning From Others   It may help you to see the variety of ways in which other organisations express their missions.

---

Bristol Cancer Centre   The Cancer Help Centre seeks to meet the needs of both cancer patient and family and to teach the patient how to channel all available energies into the process of self-healing.

**AIMS AND OBJECTIVES**
- To stimulate a positive attitude of mind and to encourage patients to help themselves.
- To offer a programme of healing for the whole person, working at the levels of body, mind and spirit.
- To provide a supportive link for cancer patients and their families and friends, with sensitive awareness of individual needs.
- To help the patient to achieve a better quality of life.

---

Harrison Cowley   David Harrison built his advertising agency from scratch first into a public company and then to become an important subsidiary of Saatchi & Saatchi. He has an excellent booklet on his approach to business, which includes his 'mission statement':

(1) To serve our clients more effectively than any other agency.

(2) To earn the respect of our clients and our industry.

(3) To maintain a highly competitive sense of urgency.

(4) To make Harrison Cowley the most agreeable, worthwhile and exciting place to work in.

(5) To maintain real and profitable growth every year.

| British Airways | Chairman, Lord King, and Chief Executive, Sir Colin Marshall, intend BA to be the best and most successful airline in the world. Their **mission** might be expressed as being:

The highest levels of service to all customers, direct and indirect. To preserve high professional and technical standards to achieve the highest levels of safety. To provide a uniform image worldwide and to maintain a specific set of standards for each clearly defined market segment.

To respond quickly and sensibly to the changing needs of present and potential customers.

To manage, operate, and market the airline in the most efficient manner.

To create a service- and people-orientated work environment.

To earn a profit sufficient to provide an acceptable return on assets. |

| Smiths Crisps | The Managing Director of Smiths Crisps defines the mission of his company as being:

- To offer consistently high quality products.
- To support existing strong brands.
- To introduce distinctive value-added new brands.
- To utilise manufacturing expertise and strengths on its extruded food items. |

| IBM | In addition to the three statements of mission

- Respect for the individual
- Service to the customer and
- Pursuit of excellence

IBM has very specific business goals:

- To enhance our customer partnerships.
- To grow as fast as the industry.
- To maintain technological and product leadership.
- To be the most efficient high volume, low cost, quality producer, marketer and administrator.
- To generate sufficient profit to sustain growth. |

# CORPORATE OBJECTIVES

Clearly, the sense of **mission** can be enlarged into a statement of corporate objectives.

Unigate

I am grateful to John Clements, the Chairman of Unigate, for permission to reproduce his own statement of corporate objectives.

The 1986 Annual Report set out certain strategic objectives which represent the internally generated success criteria against which the Group's performance is measured. However, whilst these statements set a direction for the Group, they do not provide the guidelines by which our managers should conduct and represent the business in pursuit of these objectives, nor do they reflect the responsibilities that the Group has to key interest groups. It was to fill this need that The Corporate Statement, which provides objectives of direct relevance to every business within the Group, was prepared.

## PRINCIPAL CORPORATE OBJECTIVES

In stating the principal corporate objectives, emphasis is placed on two key areas, the shareholders and the quality of earnings. In the remainder of the Corporate Statement, Unigate's responsibilities to other interest groups are recognized, but within the framework of the following:

(i) To exercise our stewardship of shareholders' interests, in a manner which maximises shareholders' wealth within our legal, moral and social obligations.

(ii) To achieve steady, well-founded growth in real earnings per share, through profitable expansion of our operations.

## OUR SHAREHOLDERS

The objectives in relation to our shareholders concentrate on their interests but also include the intention that they understand the direction of the business and are able to identify with its achievements. The specific objectives are:

(i) To take the shareholders' interests into account in key business decisions.

(ii) To communicate the corporate objectives, achievements and prospects of the business to shareholders effectively and with integrity.

## OUR CONSUMERS & CUSTOMERS

For a group with the breadth of Unigate a single marketing plan is impossible. We also recognize that the people to whom we sell our goods and services, our customers, are not always the ultimate consumers of those goods and services. However, in every market in which the Group operates our intention is to be bound by the following:

(i) To anticipate the needs of our consumers through constant innovation and development; by so doing, to succeed in maintaining and enhancing a firm business foundation with our customers.

(ii) To offer our consumers, through a balance of quality, price and service, the best value for money products and services in the market-place.

(iii) To remain close to our customers at all levels of the Group and build lasting relationships with them.

## OUR SUPPLIERS

In setting objectives for relationships with suppliers the emphasis is on the fairness of the deal:

To build and maintain a secure relationship with all of our suppliers which will ensure that:

(i) supplies are provided on time, are of the correct quality and are fairly and competitively priced.

(ii) suppliers work closely with us to ensure that the raw materials, goods and services they provide are used effectively.

(iii) suppliers are innovative in the development of products which meet our needs as customers.

## OUR EMPLOYEES

The objectives as regards our employees are a reflection of their importance:

To manage our people as the key resource in sustaining our long term competitive strength:

(i) by developing the diversity of skills and competence required in our different market sectors and at all levels of the Group.

(ii) by enhancing, through training and development, our employees' capacity for change and innovation.

(iii) by developing employees with potential, to broaden their experience, and by making use of appropriate opportunities to transfer their skills within the Group.

(iv) by maintaining competitive remuneration and benefits policies which reflect both business performance and the achievements of our staff, and by providing a standard of working environment that is valued and respected by both employees and customers.

(v) by encouraging two-way communication with our employees about our businesses and their contribution to our success so that we build a long term mutual commitment.

The Long Service Corps is an organization of people who have at one time completed forty years service with the Group and has 1,719 members. The loyalty and commitment of our employees provides Unigate with the resource to implement its decisions and attain its objectives.

## THE COMMUNITY

As a major employer, Unigate's objectives in relation to the community are as follows:

(i) To conduct our businesses in a manner which fully recognizes our responsibilities to the communities in which we operate.

(ii) To encourage employees to play an active part in local community life, both in a corporate and private capacity.

# CULTURE

People:
The Key

You and I will only achieve our **vision** through the people we employ. Just as we have our own individual personalities, so too will our company have its own personality or, to use another word, culture.

Anita Roddick stresses her commitment to enthusiasm, joy, magic, and theatre and she then carries through policies towards her colleagues and franchisees which ensure that this is the **culture** she creates to achieve her vision.

Discipline

So, the words you and I use to express our vision and our mission exert their own discipline upon us. If we stress our commitment to total customer satisfaction, we must demonstrate this commitment in everything we do and in the culture we create by the way in which we recruit, induct, train, motivate, and reward those we employ to achieve our vision.

# CREATE A CUSTOMER-SATISFYING PRODUCT OR SERVICE

That you **CREATE** a product or service which meets the needs of your target customer groups better than your competitors through your competitive **STRATEGIES**, your **DESIGN**, your organisational **STRUCTURES** and your communication **SYSTEMS**.

## SQUEEZING COSTS

The prime task of a chief executive is to provide **strategic leadership**, something at which Jan Carlzon excels.

Sagging Demand

His first chief executive role was with Vingresor, an air tour operator. The 1973–4 oil crisis had escalated air travel prices so much that passengers were not booking the tours his company provided.

Squeezing Costs

In a sagging market, most product-orientated executives would have cut back on service. But this would only bring in less revenue, creating an even more serious problem. He chose to squeeze costs: to drive cost down so that he could make a profit from fewer customers. He restructured the organisation, making it more flexible and able to handle more customers should the market recover. The market did recover. His company was able to absorb the new demand and earned the largest profit in its history.

## CREATING CUSTOMER ORIENTATION

Reduce Income!

When Jan Carlzon took over the Swedish domestic airline Linjeflyg, he needed to generate more business. 'Let's cut fares in half on those departures with low passenger loads,' he suggested.

| | |
|---|---|
| Four Point Plan | Actually, his business strategy had four points designed to convert Linjeflyg from a product-orientated company into a **customer-driven** company: |

(1) Getting more customers so his aircraft could fly more frequently with greater utilisation.

(2) Provide good service in terms of convenient timetables, frequent departures, and low prices.

(3) Give customer-facing employees more responsibility for customer satisfaction.

(4) Streamline administration.

| | |
|---|---|
| Meeting Customer Needs | His idea was to let the customers tell Linjeflyg what they wanted, and then ensure that the operations department met their needs. |
| | 'All Sweden at half price!' was a plain and simple message. He also offered standby tickets to any destination in Sweden for 100 Swedish Kroner (approximately £15). |
| | The number of passengers increased by 44 per cent and profits followed. |

# FOCUSING ON BUSINESS TRAVELLERS

| | |
|---|---|
| Destructive Cost Cutting | When Jan Carlzon took over as chief executive of SAS, the previous management had cut costs equally from all activities and all departments. In so doing, they had eliminated many services that customers wanted and were prepared to pay for, while retaining others of no interest to customers. In cutting costs in this way, the company was slicing away its own competitive strengths. |
| Focus (Step Four) | Jan Carlzon decided to focus on one group of customers: the frequent business traveller. He phased out any expense which did not help to serve business travellers. He was prepared to spend more money if it did help the business traveller. In fact, he invested an additional $45 million and increased operating expenses by $12 million a year. |
| Customers Come First | More importantly, he changed the culture of the company, and transformed employee attitudes by imbuing them with the **vision** that 'customers came first'. |

| Profits Follow | He increased earnings by nearly $80 million in the first year alone. Within 3 years he had increased the number of full-paying passengers by 23 per cent and discount passengers by 7 per cent, even though the market was stagnant. |

# STRATEGIC LEADERSHIP

| 'Helicopter Sense' | Jan Carlzon says that what is required is strategic thinking or 'helicopter sense' – a talent for rising above the details to see the lie of the land and to provide strategic leadership. |

# STRATEGIC OPTIONS

| Practical Example | Jan Carlzon demonstrated three strategic options. |
| | At Vingresor he faced a slumping market so he had to **cut costs** to make a profit on the customers available. |
| | At Linjeflyg he had fixed costs, so he had to **increase revenues**: by lowering fares and increasing the number of flights and thus increasing customer satisfaction. |
| | At SAS he provided **added value** by differentiating the service he provided to one specific customer group, or segment, the business traveller. |

| Three Options | Every business has the same three options in seeking to evolve a competitive strategy:
  - Added-value/differentiation
  - Volume
  - Costs. |

| Only One Option? | The Strategic Planning Institute in Cambridge, Massachusetts, has the largest strategic database in the world, called Profit Impact of Marketing Strategy (PIMS). It has studied the accounts of thousands of companies to work out – on a large computer database – which marketing strategies achieve the best financial results. |

| Perceived Product Quality | 'The single variable far and away the most closely associated with good financial performance over the long haul', it says, 'is **perceived product quality.**' |

| | |
|---|---|
| Start from Quality | Note that the **perception** is that of the customers. Successful companies put perception of customers very high in their considerations. Losers, they say, 'downgrade the customer's views'. |
| | PIMS goes on to say, 'First achieve a relative perceived product quality edge over your competitors. If you do, you will gain share. Then take advantage of economies of scale. Start from quality, achieve low costs as a result.' |
| | Hence the order in which I have put the three strategic options. If we accept the advice of PIMS, we have only one strategic option: |

(1) Start with quality, with added value, by differentiating your product or service in the perceptions of your customers.

(2) If you succeed, you will gain market share and develop volume.

(3) If you develop volume, you can cover your costs and start to improve your margin of profit. Not that this should stop you seeking creative ways of cutting costs in any event.

| | |
|---|---|
| Focus | As we have agreed when discussing Steps Three, Four, and Five, all these strategies need to be related to specific groups or segments of customers. |

## ADDED VALUE: DIFFERENTIATION

| | |
|---|---|
| Product-led, Price-driven | Many introverted companies are preoccupied with the product they produce or the service they provide. Since they are preoccupied with **what** they do, they become deeply preoccupied with price. In the absence of creative thinking, they are forced into believing that all customers buy only on price, when only subsistence segments do so. |
| Value for Money | For top end segments this is a fallacy. Do you, or your wife, buy the cheapest possible toilet paper, write with the cheapest biro, stay in the cheapest hotel, or drive the cheapest car? The answer is no! We seek to enhance the quality of our life by ensuring that we derive value from our money. |
| M & S | Marks & Spencer does not sell on price, but on added value. |

| Mothercare | Remember the Mothercare example. The previous owner had striven to sell more and more prams at lower and lower prices. His successor set about creating an added value service to mothers in the concept of 'Mothercare', which enabled him to enhance margins. |
|---|---|
| With Extras:<br>Without Extras | When we come to discuss the way in which you design your product or service, you will see that you have two options when seeking to 'add value'. |

As we saw with the oil engineer, he didn't really sell a valve, he sold a complete advisory service.

Just providing the intangibles which customers value, such as speed, reassurance, convenience, courtesy, and cheerfulness, can be one way of 'adding value' to your product or service.

The second way of 'adding value' is – paradoxically – to cut away the trimmings. If all your competitors force your customers to buy a complete 'package', perhaps you can gain an advantage by merely supplying your customers with the essential elements of what they need.

# VOLUME

If we accept the advice of PIMS, we will put quality first and allow volume to follow.

We have all read of the disasters of tour operators seeking to work on low cost, high volumes. Perhaps Sir Freddie Laker's problem was that to retain customers he had to start to 'add value' which destroyed his cost structures.

# CREATIVE COST REDUCTION

| Destructive<br>Methods | We have all known of companies which issue an edict that every department must cut costs by 10 per cent. As we have seen, Jan Carlzon's solution was to cut every cost which did not help to serve customers, but to increase costs which did serve customers. |
|---|---|
| The Body<br>Shop | Before the arrival of The Body Shop, most women had had a sneaking suspicion that the way in which their cosmetics were packaged cost far more than the cosmetics themselves. The Body Shop demonstrated both its **vision** of honesty and its **mission** by using low-cost, refillable, and/or recyclable packaging materials. |

| Making 'Individual' Cranes | The fact that one should put 'added value' first does not mean that we should not try to gain a competitive advantage by creative methods of reducing costs. |
|---|---|

Pre-costed Components

The *Industrial Marketing Digest* mentions a crane-making company which was facing intense price competition in a stagnant market. At that time, cranes were made by traditional 'metal-bashing' methods. The company designed a set of components from which a wide range of cranes could be assembled to the precise specification requested by a customer.

Because each element was pre-costed, a fully detailed quotation could be submitted promptly to every potential customer, while competitors were still struggling to work out costs. Equally, the company could promise delivery almost from stock, whereas competitors, if they gained the order, would then have to start 'metal bashing'.

Competitive Advantage

Hence the company gained a competitive advantage in speed of quotations, speed of delivery, and earned increased profits.

## EVOLVING YOUR STRATEGY

Competitive Strategy
Competitive Advantage

Harvard professor Michael Porter has written two major books, *Competitive Strategy* and *Competitive Advantage*. He argues that it is difficult to gain a competitive advantage by looking at a firm as a whole. He breaks a firm down into what he calls its 'value chain', as illustrated.

A value chain diagram (shaped as a house with "MARGIN" along the roof). The contents:

**Support Activities**

| | Inbound Logistics | Operations | Outbound Logistics | Marketing & Sales | Service |
|---|---|---|---|---|---|
| **FIRM INFRASTRUCTURE** | Top Management Support in Selling — Facilities that Enhance the Firm's Image — Superior Management Information System (spanning across) | | | | |
| **HUMAN RESOURCE MANAGEMENT** | Superior Training of Personnel | Stable Workforce Policies; Quality of Work Life Programs; Programs to Attract the Best Scientists and Engineers | | Sales Incentives to Retain Best Salespersons; Recruiting Better Qualified Sales and Service Personnel | Extensive Training of Service Technicians |
| **TECHNOLOGY DEVELOPMENT** | Superior Material Handling & Sorting Technology; Proprietary Quality Assurance Equipment | Unique Product Features; Rapid Model Introductions; Unique Production Process or Machines; Automated Inspection Procedures | Unique Vehicle Scheduling Software; Special Purpose Vehicles or Containers | Applications Engineering Support; Superior Media Research; Most Rapid Quotations for Tailored Models | Advanced Servicing Techniques |
| **PROCUREMENT** | Most Reliable Transportation for Inbound Deliveries | Highest Quality Raw Materials; Highest Quality Components | Best Located Warehouses; Transportation Suppliers that Minimize Damage | Most Desirable Media Placements; Product Positioning and Image | High Quality Replacement Parts |

**Primary Activities**

| Inbound Logistics | Operations | Outbound Logistics | Marketing & Sales | Service |
|---|---|---|---|---|
| Handling of Inputs that Minimizes Damage or Degradation; Timeliness of Supply to the Manufacturing Process | Tight Conformance to Specifications; Attractive Product Appearance; Responsiveness to Specification Changes; Low Defect Rates; Short Time to Manufacture | Rapid and Timely Delivery; Accurate and Responsive Order Processing; Handling that Minimizes Damage | High Advertising Level and Quality; High Sales Force Coverage and Quality; Personal Relationships with Channels or Buyers; Superior Technical Literature & Other Sales Aids; Most Extensive Promotion; Most Extensive Credit to Buyers or Channels | Rapid Installation; High Service Quality; Complete Field Stocking of Replacement Parts; Wide Service Coverage; Extensive Buyer Training |

| | |
|---|---|
| Primary Activities | These Michael Porter describes as being: |

- **Inbound Logistics.** Activities associated with the receiving, storing and providing of goods, including materials. Handling, warehousing, inventory control, scheduling, and returns to suppliers.

- **Operation.** Activities associated with transforming inputs into the final platform, such as machining, assembling, packaging, equipment maintenance, testing, and facility operations.

- **Outbound Logistics.** Activities associated with collecting, storing, and physically distributing products to buyers, including warehousing, material handling, delivery vehicle operation, order processing and scheduling.

- **Marketing and Sales.** Activities associated with providing the means by which buyers can purchase your product or service and inducing them to do so, such as advertising, promotion, sales forces, quotation services, channels of distribution (agents, distributors, dealers) and pricing.

- **Service.** Activities associated with providing a service to enhance or maintain the value of the product, such as installation, repair, training, parts supply, and warranties.

| | |
|---|---|
| Support Activities | These Michael Porter breaks down under four headings: |

- **Procurement.** This refers to the function of purchasing the goods and services you need for your production services.

- **Technology Development.** The range of activities which relate to efforts to improve the product and the process of production.

- **Human Resource Management.** Activities involving recruiting, hiring, training, motivating and developing every level of employee.

- **Infrastructure.** Activities which include general management, planning, finance, accounting, legal, government affairs and management of quality.

| | |
|---|---|
| Advantages of Value Chains | The great advantage claimed for a value chain is that it splits a firm into strategic relevant activities, to help recognise existing or potential ways of 'adding value' or reducing costs. |

Cost Advantage   A company may be able to achieve a cost advantage from primary activities such as:

- a low-cost physical distribution system
- a highly efficient assembly process, or
- a highly productive sales forces.

Added Value/   A company may be able to differentiate its product or supply added
Differentiation   value to its customers by:

- buying better quality raw materials
- designing a better product or service, or
- having a very fast and responsive quotation service.

Linkages   One of the problems of conventional accountancy is that it can sometimes focus attention on the wrong statistics.

Michael Porter describes linkages as the relationship between the way in which one value activity is performed and the impact this has on the cost or performance of another.

Buying high-quality pre-cut steel sheets can simplify and speed manufacturing and minimise wastage.

A more costly product design, more stringent material purchase specifications, and greater in-process inspection may produce a product with little or no post-purchase warranty costs. And, in the process, attract and satisfy more customers, pleased with greater reliability.

An inter-active order entry system will not only involve the customer in the reordering process, but help manufacturing scheduling and sales force utilisation.

Conventional management accounts would find it difficult to allocate the cost and the benefits between the departments concerned.

Using Value   • **Suppliers.** Close co-operation with your suppliers may enable
Chains   both of you to benefit. Thus, the relationships which Marks & Spencer has created with its suppliers is undoubtedly beneficial to both parties and – in addition – creates one of the competitive advantages which M & S has secured for itself with its customers.

133

- **Competitors.** The value chain conceptualises a more objective way of assessing your competitors and, by studying every aspect of their primary and supportive activities, you can better relate their operation to your own in a way which enables you to secure a competitive advantage.

- **Segmentation.** Selecting only one particular group of customers or industry segment to serve may enable you to tailor your value chain to that group of customers, and thus achieve lower costs, or differentiation in serving this customer segment compared to competitors.

- **Diversification.** Finally, studying your own value chain carefully may enable you to recognise opportunities for diversification. An example of this we saw with Edgar Vaughan once it realised that its strength was enhancing the production process of its customers.

# CONCLUSION

While Professor Porter, like every expert, has his own technical language, he is really talking plain common sense.

The more we understand about our customers, our competitors, and ourselves, the better able shall we be to succeed. His 'value chain' is no more than a common-sense way of looking at how your company and your competitors react to customers and suppliers.

The concept is helpful in terms of looking at strategy, which should be based on:

- Adding value to customers.

If, in the process, it helps us to reduce our operating costs and to improve our profit margins, we shall be better able to serve our customers.

# STEP SEVEN: DESIGNING YOUR PRODUCT OR SERVICE

## DESIGN

Winning Ways  One of the best books I have read on the subject is *Winning Ways*, written by one of the leading experts in the subject, James Pilditch, who discusses how 'winning' companies create the products which customers want to buy.

*Denford's low-cost Computer Aided Design training packages bring advanced technology within school and college budgets, using existing BBC/Acorn micro-computers.*

Design Council  If you do feel you need help, this is available from the Design Council. One of its award-winning companies made a device to seal the plastic bags which are now in common use for many products.

The Design Council's engineers were able to suggest methods of laser profiling cutting which halved fabrication costs and were also able to help with things like new paint finishes and the sourcing of marketing control panels, neither of which the company had been aware of.

So, however good you and your team of experts may be, it can always be worthwhile to get an objective view on what you are doing.

| | |
|---|---|
| Customers' Viewpoint | It is particularly important to get objective help in viewing your product or service **from the point of view of the customer**. |
| | It might be helpful to discuss some of these areas of **'customer presentation'** together. |

# BUNDLING

| | |
|---|---|
| What it Means | I do not like using technical terms, but since other people use them, I can't escape mentioning them to you. One trend you may have seen in your own experience is the way in which companies seek to provide an all-embracing comprehensive service for customers. This is called 'bundling'. |
| One-Stop Shopping | One aspect of this is the development of one-stop shopping, first pioneered so brilliantly by Mothercare. |
| | Banks, too, are broadening the range of services they provide, including the Black Horse Estate Agency. |
| Use of Product | As private individuals, we like to own our possessions. Commercial organisations, particularly those with limited finance, are more concerned with gaining the use of facilities. A member of the Finance Houses Association will be able to provide you with the finance and the appropriate scheme you need to be able to hire or lease your product to your customers. |
| Extending Customer Base | In so doing, you may be able to extend the number of customers able to use your product or services. |
| Management Service | You will be aware that you can 'contract hire' vehicles. When you do, you gain a complete 'management service' – the vehicles are serviced, maintained, and repaired, and, if necessary, you are provided with a replacement vehicle. Rightly, the supplying company makes a profit, not only from the vehicle itself but from providing the labour, parts, insurance, and other elements of the service it is providing. |
| | You may be able to provide similar 'contract hire' facilities to your customers, and in so doing earn additional profits, from the additional services provided as part of the 'package'. |

| | |
|---|---|
| Benefits of Product | Edgar Vaughan's decided that it was not in the business of selling oils but was a 'partner' in the production processes of its customers. It therefore supported its customers with sales executives able to give advice on how to improve and enhance production. |
| | Building in advice of this sort is another way of enhancing the value of your product or service to your customers. Thus Ciba-Geigy does not merely sell farm fertilisers but employs qualified graduates able to give money-making, money-saving advice to farmers. |
| 'Hassle'-free Experience | Many individual customers lack either experience or confidence or both. As Theodore Levitt has said, 'They are looking for a comfortable "commercial womb" which will look after them, and provide them with a "hassle-free" experience.' |
| | While business executives may have more confidence in themselves, they tend to work under pressure. They, too, want a 'hassle-free' buying experience. |
| | The more we can do to make life easier for our customers by providing a comprehensive service, the more customers we will gain, together with a greater opportunity to earn a fair profit from the increased range of services we are providing. |
| Your 'Core' Business | However, there is a danger that by so doing you may become 'jack of all trades, and master of none'. |
| | Woolworths has recognised that it needs to re-focus what it does and is now going to concentrate on six product ranges. |
| | As companies grow, they too tend to accumulate too many activities, with the result that they lose their way, and lose their 'vision'. |
| | George Turnbull has done a brilliant job in slimming down the worldwide Inchcape Group from an unwieldy total of some thirty activities to a more logical grouping of ten, of which five are regarded as being the 'core' businesses, which will receive particular emphasis in terms of investment. |
| | Even quite small companies can generate a 'hotch-potch' of activities and thus lose the sense of vision and mission of their early years. |
| | It is very important to concentrate on the 'core' activities of your **vision**. |

# UNBUNDLING

Specialist
Activities

Indeed, there are those who feel that specialisation pays, and that focusing on a very limited range of activities is the key to success. Classic examples in retailing are the 'Tie Rack', 'Sock Shop', and 'Knobs & Knockers'.

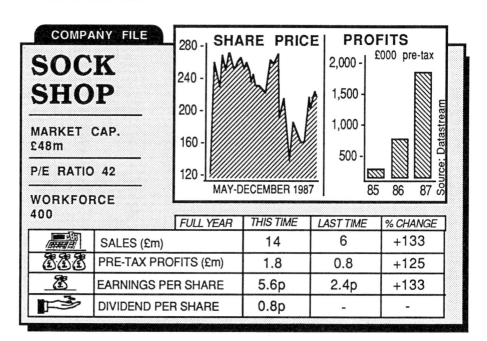

| FULL YEAR | | THIS TIME | LAST TIME | % CHANGE |
|---|---|---|---|---|
| | SALES (£m) | 14 | 6 | +133 |
| | PRE-TAX PROFITS (£m) | 1.8 | 0.8 | +125 |
| | EARNINGS PER SHARE | 5.6p | 2.4p | +133 |
| | DIVIDEND PER SHARE | 0.8p | - | - |

Customer
Resentment

Some customers are beginning to resent being dragooned into buying a comprehensive service when all they want is one aspect of the service or product.

You will have seen a new generation of hotels being developed, often located near motorway junctions, which are concentrating on meeting the specific needs of business travellers without all the extras normally provided for holidaymakers.

'Unbundling'

So we come to even uglier expression of 'unbundling'. Companies are being successful by deleting stages of production and features of their service that their customers do not need.

Half-made
Products

A paper mill was finding competition difficult. Because it was in a salt water estuary, its effluent problems were not as severe as its competitors. It stopped making paper but started to produce half-made paper, which it sold to its former competitors. The advantage to its competitors was that it reduced effluent problems.

Other chemical companies have found that, instead of waiting for the completion of every stage of their production processes, some customers prefer to buy at one of the intermediate stages.

# PACKAGING

The Body Shop

When Anita Roddick started The Body Shop, she turned her lack of funds into a benefit. She sold her products in five different sizes of bottle. She used low-cost labels and focused the attention of her customers on the product and not its packaging.

Creating Confidence

Customers do not like being made to feel ignorant. It is said, for example, that young ladies do not like to buy joints of meat from an 'old fashioned' butcher, because they do not understand the different cuts. They prefer to buy a joint of meat from the supermarket, pre-priced and pre-packaged.

Important Aspect

So, the way in which you package your product is important.

Do some test marketing. Take a few of your colleagues into a Payless or a B & Q and get them to mark out of ten those products to which they instinctively reach, and those they tend to overlook.

# DO YOUR CUSTOMERS OPTIMISE BENEFITS?

Transferring Your Expertise

You and your sales team may be convinced that your product benefits your customers. One reason for your confidence will be that you have lived with the product and service for so long that you can 'make it sing'.

Insecure Customers

Your customers will not have had the benefit of all this experience, and may not be able to derive maximum value from your product. They may make pleasant noises because they are reasonably satisfied but – unknown to you – they may not be getting the full benefit that they should, and will thus be open to the blandishments of a competitive salesman.

Third-party Customers

Equally important, if your equipment has to be used by operatives, they will become 'third-party customers'. Their reactions may well influence whether or not you gain repeat orders. (Hauliers often consult their drivers when deciding to buy another lorry, as one example.) So, making sure that your direct and third-party customers truly benefit from your product or service is an important element in your design.

User Manuals

How many times has your wife bought a new vacuum cleaner, washing machine, or other item of household equipment and then sought your help in finding out how to use it?

How many times have you, like me, got bad tempered at trying to understand the somewhat incomprehensible instructions. Frequently, the manuals seem to cover more than one model, and the instructions relate to features which are lacking from the model my wife happens to have purchased.

Frustration all round!

Too often these manuals seem to be regarded as an afterthought, when in fact they should be carefully designed as part of the product or service you are providing to your customers.

User Training

Similarly, if you are selling a complex product, it is vital to ensure that your customer, or, more accurately, his operatives, can derive the optimum value from the purchase.

Customer Support Services

Adequate pre-installation training, careful coaching on the installation equipment, and the adequacy of post-installation problem-solving and retraining will all be essential elements in the design of your product.

Companies which really place emphasis on customer support services can secure a distinct competitive advantage.

## DON'T FORGET THE CUSTOMER!

Customers, Not Hardware

Product-led companies are very keen to make better machines, sometimes with no thought as to whether their machines will provide a genuine improvement in meeting customer needs.

New Aircraft

When Jan Carlzon took charge of SAS he found it had just spent $120 million on four new Airbuses, with a further eight on order.

140

These aircraft could be operated 6 per cent more cheaply per passenger mile than the existing DC9s, providing they were full. They had 240 seats. The DC9s had 110 seats.

Reduced
Customer
Benefits

So, the only way in which the new aircraft could be made profitable would be to slash the timetable, with fewer flights, and so provide a much lower standard of service to customers.

Aircraft
Mothballed

Jan Carlzon decided to mothball the new aircraft and to continue using the existing DC9s, which enabled him to provide customers with more frequent services.

Meet Customer
Needs

Make sure that all your **design** activities are focused on meeting the needs and wants of your customers, or enable your customers to meet the needs and wants of their customers.

# STEP SEVEN: DESIGNING A CUSTOMER-SATISFYING ORGANISATION

**Objective of Business**

The first and only task of any business is to identify, attract, satisfy, and retain customers.

**Organisation**

It therefore seems only common sense that every business should be organised in such a way as to facilitate the achievement of this objective.

**Common Sense Ignored**

Yet common sense is ignored in many business organisations.

Typically an organisation is organised to produce, to account, to administer, and to sell what has been produced.

Very few organisations have been organised to identify, attract, satisfy, and retain customers.

**Lack of Skills**

I know of many companies who do not employ a single manager with the skills needed to carry out these four priority tasks.

**Lack of Measurement**

The lack of focus on customer-orientated measurements such as:

- Customer Perception Index
- Customer Satisfaction Index
- Customer Retention Index

indicates that many management control systems do not even consider the need to address the central purpose of finding and keeping customers.

**Flattening the Pyramid**

Let's go back to Jan Carlzon's comment on this point:

'Any business organisation seeking to establish customer orientation must flatten the pyramid – that is, eliminate the hierarchical tiers of responsibility to respond directly and quickly to customer's needs.

'Managing is thus shifted from the executive suite to the operational level where everyone is now a manager of his own situation. When problems arise, each employee has the authority to analyse the situation, determine the appropriate action, and see to it that the action (to satisfy customers) is carried out, either alone or with the help of others.'

| | |
|---|---|
| **Lost: Middle Management?** | Jan Carlzon honestly admits that this created problems for his middle management. Customer-facing employees were enthusiastic about the additional responsibility they had been given to manage their own relationships with their customers.

Top managers were equally enthusiastic in their role as visionaries and as missionaries. |

**Reversal of Roles**

But middle managers were confused and frustrated. Previously their job had been to make sure that their subordinates obeyed the rules. Now customer-facing employees were being encouraged to break the rules to make sure that customers were satisfied.

**New Skills Needed**

'To motivate the front line and support their efforts required skilled, knowledgeable middle managers who are proficient at coaching, informing, criticising, praising, educating, and so forth. Their authority applies to . . . mobilising the necessary resources for the front line to achieve their objectives.'

**Managing Up**

When Sir Colin Marshall of British Airways spoke at one of our client meetings, he too stressed that 'the job of good managers is to teach, to motivate, and to act as a role model so that others may find better ways to perform'.

At British Airways he, like Jan Carlzon, has invested heavily to finance a programme of change by total involvement.

**Lousy Service**

In his typical forthright style, Jim Maxmin of Thorn EMI said – again at one of our client meetings –

'. . . the lousy service we offer, or the failure to achieve market share, is actually encouraged by the nature of the organisations and management styles we have'.

He continued,

'Ask yourself the question, if there is bad or indifferent interaction between customers and employees – why? The answer must be the **organisation** which we have created.'

| | |
|---|---|
| Bottom-down Organisation | What these outstandingly successful business executives are saying is that far greater responsibility must be given to our customer-facing employees. |
| Upturning Organisation Charts | In future, you will need to draw your organisation's chart as an upturned pyramid.

The top tier will be the members of your organisation who are in direct contact with your customers.

The second tier will be those supplying the resources needed by those in contact with customers.

The bottom tier will be you and your senior executives who are responsible for providing the sense of vision, mission, and creating the culture needed by your employees, suppliers, and customers. |

| | |
|---|---|
| Role of Senior Management | For this to happen we, as senior executives, must have a sense of **vision**, a clearly defined **mission** and should act as missionaries in making sure that everyone in the company understands what we are seeking to achieve. |
| Role of Middle Management | The role of middle management is then to assist front-line customer-facing employees. First, as motivators and teachers and, secondly, by making sure that they have the resources they need to satisfy our customers. |
| Demanding | As Sir Colin Marshall observed at our meeting, this change to total involvement is very demanding on senior executives, on middle management, and on customer-facing employees. It is very expensive, but, as he observed, it is a way of solidly underwriting the future of any organisation.

We will return in more detail to this topic in a future book in this series. |

# CASE STUDY: SALES ORGANISATION

KALAMAWHO? When Bill Nickoll joined Kalamazoo business systems as managing director, at the invitation of chairman Tom Garnier last year, he conducted a cheeky little experiment. He asked a friend to phone Kalamazoo, enquiring after office systems. Round came a salesman, who gave a very professional presentation on business forms (one of Kalamazoo's leading products). Nickoll's friend then mentioned installing a computer. Kalamazoo is Britain's third-largest micro-distributor; has a team of 90 software programmers; and employs experts in computer maintenance, technical training and the like. But the salesman drew in his breath: 'Computers are bad news,' he warned. When a computer systems salesman was eventually coaxed out of the company, the process was repeated in reverse. 'Ooh, you don't want to touch forms,' said he (although the use of forms, Nickoll points out, actually increases with computers). This proof of a 'segmented sales organization' gave Nickoll a clue as to why Kalamazoo's 180,000 customers (more than IBM UK) were spending only an average £250 a year. So, instead of recommending new products or acquisitions to rescue the loss-making Kalamazoo, Nicholl restructured the selling organization 'to expose ourselves to the dangers of sale'. Those 180,000 customers are now treated as accounts; specialist forces now target vertical markets like the motor trade; quotas have been doubled (and achieved); and Kalamazoo is back in profit.

*Reproduced with kind permission of* Management Today.

# STEP SEVEN: CREATING CUSTOMER-SATISFYING SYSTEMS

Customer Relations

Your relations with your customers are affected by the **systems** you employ. At the most basic, this is a pad which ensures that all messages from customers are received, logged, and actioned. At the more technologically advanced end of the scale, it is an appropriate electronic system which enables your computer to send and receive information to and from the computer of your customers and suppliers without paper.

Move Planes, Not Customers

Early one morning Jan Carlzon arrived at Copenhagen airport from New York and had to change planes to get to Stockholm. He was tired from flying all night, and had plenty of hand luggage. He was told he had to walk half a mile to another terminal building.

When he asked why, he was told it was more convenient to tow the aeroplanes to the gate nearest the hangar in which they had been serviced. He continues:

'I've heard many business travellers swear about having to rush around between the concourses – but I have never heard an aeroplane complain about being towed a couple of hundred yards. Today at Copenhagen we tow planes from concourse to concourse. Whereas once two-thirds of our passengers in transit had to change concourses at Copenhagen, that figure is down to one-third. Not only are our passengers less harried, but we have minimised delays caused by waiting for passengers who needed to dash from one concourse to another.'

Inconvenience to **Customers**

**'As I learned more about SAS I was amazed at how many of its policies and procedures catered to the equipment or the employees, even if they inconvenienced the passengers! Equally amazing was how easy these practices were to spot – and to rectify – by looking at them from the point of view of our target customer, the frequent business traveller.'**

Mystery Shopping

One of the most valuable techniques any business can use is to employ 'mystery shoppers'. There are organisations, including my own, which do this for companies on a professional basis.

We ring up a company to record how long it takes them to answer the phone, ensure that we are transferred to the right department, and then assess how well or badly our enquiry is handled.

We actually go into companies with 'mystery shoppers' authorised to buy the product or service concerned to see how well or badly the sale is handled.

If you are running a small company, you can probably do this informally by asking some of your friends to do it on your behalf. But if it is to be done on a regular basis, then it needs to be done professionally.

## Making it Easy to Buy

How easy do you make it for your customers to buy from you?

No, it's not a stupid question. It is surprising how many organisations make it tremendously difficult for customers to buy.

## Attitude Training

This is why SAS, British Airways, Audi Volkswagen, and many other outstandingly successful companies invest so heavily in training every employee and executive in customer-facing skills.

When we carry out this training, we ask that executives and employees from every different department and location of the business are mixed in together so that they can see how they all inter-relate. We find this encourages a far more constructive approach towards inter-departmental co-operation, instead of – as so often happens – inter-departmental conflict.

## Achieving Vision: Mission

If we are to achieve our objective, to fulfil our vision and to implement our mission, we need to have a system that will enable us to carry out every activity in relation to identifying, attracting, satisfying, and retaining customers . . . profitably.

Inevitably, this will mean that we need to buy a computer on which to build our total customer/prospect database.

As we grow, this basic customer communication database needs to be incorporated into other systems related to the ways in which our customers order, receive, and pay for the goods and services they are buying from us.

In this way, the right systems can give us a competitive advantage.

| Customer | Retailers selling Hotpoint products have been given an interactive |
|---|---|
| Orders | computer terminal – using an Istel System – which means that for the |

Customer
Orders

Retailers selling Hotpoint products have been given an interactive computer terminal – using an Istel System – which means that for the cost of a local phone call, the customer can interrogate the interactive system to specify the precise model he or she wants to buy. Once the customer has finished specifying his or her order, it is sent down the computer line to the factory and used to schedule the manufacturing, ordering, and delivery processes.

Invoicing
Customers

When Tom Farmer's Kwik-Fit operation works on a car belonging to a large fleet operator, it does not send an invoice. That evening Tom's computer transfers the details of the transaction to the computer of the fleet company concerned.

It is a totally immediate, paperless transaction. It helps the customer to have immediate information about the work that has been done on his car. It helps Tom to immediately invoice the customer, who will then arrange for his computer to credit Tom's bank account.

EPOS

The EPOS (Electronic Point of Sale) revolution is putting the most reliable and accessible information firmly in the hands of the retailers. The larger networks such as Sainsburys have stated that by 1990 over half their sales will be through outlets operating with EPOS. Information on profit by product line is available to the retailers – manufacturers must adapt.

148

# CASE STUDY: IMPACT OF SYSTEMS

CONSIDER W.H. Smith's Holborn branch, on the edge of London's financial district. It is a distinctive store which reflects the commitment of the UK's largest bookseller and newsagent to design as good business practice. It is also a showpiece for the company's innovative approach to two retailing technologies – electronic point of sale (Epos) at the checkouts and computer-aided design (CAD) for internal store design.

WHS is already a leader, in its own market segments at any rate, in both these retailing innovations. By bringing them together the company is on the brink of creating a marketing advantage that other retailers may find hard to match.

The system it is creating will enable it not only to design each of its nearly 400 stores quickly and for maximised profitability but also to rejig stores to exploit every square metre in each store to the full.

It has committed £250,000 over the next 12 months to forging a link between Epos and CAD. Experts agree that if WHS can successfully link the two systems – and technically there seems no reason why it should not – it will have pulled off a spectacular coup.

At its most graphic, the system will enable WHS strategists to create, on a computer terminal screen, a three dimensional image of the interior of any of their 365 UK stores. They will be able to alter the internal design at will, seeking the best positions for bookshelves and record bins.

They will be able to create images of customers – men, women and children – browsing through the merchandise. They will be able to analyse how their electronic doppelgangers 'see' and are attracted to the goods on display. A child, after all, has a physically different viewpoint from an adult as does a man from a woman.

If that was all WHS could do, it would be remarkable but not sensational; designers and architects can use computers to produce stunning graphics routinely these days.

But it will also be able, through a 'bridge' to its Epos system, to incorporate the value of every product line into its electronic images. It will be able to attach a 'selling value' to every square metre of the interior of its stores, allowing it to maximise its use of space with a degree of accuracy never possible before.

*Reproduced with permission of* Financial Times.

# STEP SEVEN: CHANNELS TO REACH CUSTOMERS

Question?

What will be the most effective method of reaching your customers . . . from the viewpoint of your customers?

Direct Selling

One option is to sell direct to your own customers by one of five techniques:

- **Telephone Selling,** where you have a team phoning your customers for orders on a regular basis.

- **Direct Mail,** where you send brochures and order forms with a covering letter to encourage orders.

- **Direct Response,** where you place adverts which incorporate an order form of the type you will see every week in the Sunday colour supplements.

- **Direct Selling,** where you employ your own sales people to call on customers to collect orders.

- **Shop/Counter Sales,** where you operate your own retail shops, cash and carry style warehouses, or have trade counters in a depot.

Channels

Alternatively, you may decide to use intermediaries to help you to get your product or service to the end-user. Depending on your trade or industry, these may have different descriptions and varying terms of business, but the normal categorisation is as below:

- **Distributors.** You appoint a company to represent your interests, often in a defined market area. It agrees to hold adequate stocks, to follow your systems, including your promotions, and to train first its own staff and, if necessary, the staff employed by the dealers it may supply. In return for these contractual commitments, it receives a high level of discount.

- **Wholesalers.** They do not enter into any contractual relationships, but merely receive bulk quantity terms when they buy in sufficiently large volume from you.

- **Dealers.** Again there is a contractual relationship – possibly involving exclusivity – where they agree to hold minimum stock levels, to train their staff, and to follow your promotions. They normally buy their supplies from your local distributor, who takes responsibility for managing the dealers in his territory.
- **Retailers/Stockists.** People who happen to sell your products but have no contractual relationship to do so. They will probably buy from wholesalers or your local dealers.

Franchising

The Body Shop wanted to expand, but lacked the funds to do so. It was among the first to take advantage of the concept of franchising. It had people applying for its franchise. Initially it was delighted to help and to supply them with its products. Later it became more formalised and potential applicants had to pay a franchise fee, though The Body Shop still keeps this at a relatively nominal amount and relies on earning its income from selling the supplies franchisees need. Franchising is still in its infancy. It is governed by a 'code of practice' but many companies have found that it is difficult to find entrepreneurial franchisees able to 'grow' their own business.

Management Tasks

Making effective use of your channels of distribution is a skilled task.

Customers Come First

Whatever route you decide to take, you must remember that your **'customers come first'**. If you decide to sell direct, you need to ensure that every member of your direct sales team is totally orientated to customer satisfaction. If you decide to use one of the channels of distribution, you need to ensure that the chief executives of those you appoint share your **vision**.

# BMW CASE STUDY

**Strong Dealer Network**

While much of the success of BMW is due to brilliant positioning, another factor has been the efforts they have devoted to developing their dealers.

Dealer profit margins were sustained by offering basic models at the competitive price and offering 'extras' to customers who were willing to pay.

The dealer network was kept at 150 allowing increased sales per dealership. By concentrating on key dealerships, BMW GB were able to show how increased investment in property and facilities would be worthwhile. They now enjoy around a 90 per cent exclusive network.

Marketing communication has placed great emphasis on the BMW brand and not on individual models. Invariably it is the 7 series flagship which focuses in national advertising providing continued perceived exclusivity and drawing on customers' aspirations.

As sales have neared targeted levels the marketing message plays on the existing owners of BMW products providing a brief glimpse to non-owners at what could be in store for them.

Needless to say, the BMW story has been a huge success.

# STEP SEVEN: LOCATIONS CUSTOMERS NEED

**Successful Retailing**

It has been said that successful retailing depends on three factors. These are location, location, and location. So, what is the right location for your business?

Increasingly, as you know yourself, the car is a dominant factor in the shopping we do. Thus, convenience in terms of access and – as importantly – in terms of carparking is vital.

*Detailed Maps of many towns are available from Commercial Sources.*

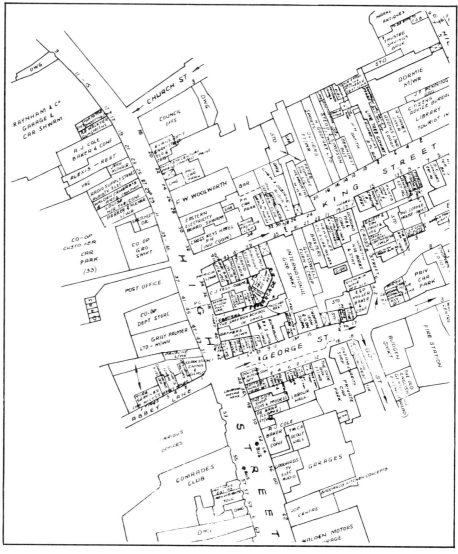

| | |
|---|---|
| **High Street Deserted?** | We are really coming back to Step Two in terms of studying the influences on the future of business. The Henley Centre for Forecasting sees the growth in out-of-town shopping areas, and the move away from the High Street. |
| **Marks & Spencer** | Hitherto, Marks & Spencer appears to have been a firm advocate of High Street shopping. But it has taken space in the new Metrocentre at Gateshead, and has announced plans for an out-of-town location in Northern Ireland. |
| **Successful Retailers** | Certainly, highly successful retailing organisations like Toys R Us, B & Q, Sainsbury's Homebase, Payless, and Do It All have all demonstrated that customers will travel for the right retailing location, with an adequate carpark and a depth and breadth of stock in a pleasant retailing ambience. |
| **Hotels** | These principles apply to hotels. We organise a lot of client meetings. We choose locations close to motorway exits, with adequate carparking. |
| **Questions?** | How does location affect the way in which you and your wife do your shopping or your leisure activities? |
| | How does location affect the way in which you buy supplies for your business? |
| | Have you asked your customers how convenient they find it to call upon you? |
| | Have you chosen the right location? |
| **The 'Right' Chimney Pots** | When we were discussing the way in which you can sub-divide your customers in Step Four, we mentioned ACORN. We agreed that counting the number of chimney pots was pointless. What matters is whether there are enough customers of the right sort to provide the sales you need. |

# CASE STUDIES ON LOCATION PLANNING

The practical uses of ACORN was covered in a Conference organised by CACI. A synopsis of three of the papers is a given below.

**TSB Branch Network**

Setting objectives for a branch network as complicated as that operated by the TSB was tackled by modelling market potential and current geographical penetration for each branch. Using ACORN statistics, the TSB and CACI were able to issue objectives and budgets based on the TSB customer profile and local demographics.

Surveys of staff acceptance of the budget and plans showed a high level of commitment due to the local content of the analysis.

Speaker: John Warner, TSB's Marketing Planning Manager

**Boots**

Understanding the customer base in a particular store's catchment area has led Boots to achieve increased sales. Using Family Expenditure Survey data in conjunction with CACI's ACORN statistics, Boots have been able to attach potential not just to individual store, but by individual department in that store.

Stores with similar customer catchments can then be compared. New stores layout or existing location refits can be targeted according to local demographic data.

Speaker: Kenneth Parsons, Operations Information Manager

**Woolworths**

The demand model used by Woolworths uses ACORN data to examine the customer profile in each location. This enables the right footage to be allocated to 'Focus Product Ranges' thereby attempting to maximize sales and profiles for each store.

Speaker: Graham Wallace

<table>
<tr><td>

**8**

</td><td>

## ATTRACTING CUSTOMERS

That you **ATTRACT** an increasing number of customers by the way in which you **POSITION** yourself to create the right **PERCEPTIONS** in the minds of your customers, and through a sustained series of **PROMOTIONS** both to your direct customers, and those able to influence their decision to buy from you.

</td></tr>
</table>

## CREATING YOUR MARKETING 'PLATFORM'

| | |
|---|---|
| Gaining a 'Window' | Customers are bombarded by thousands of advertising messages every day on TV; on the radio; on the sides of buses, taxis, lorries; on hoardings; in their post, newspapers, and magazines; and even on parking meters! So, to get your message across, you have to find a way of opening a 'window' for your product or service in the minds of your customers. |
| Perception | 'Perception is truth to the perceiver.' The way in which you and your company and its products or services are perceived by your customers or clients may be totally inaccurate, but these perceptions are the 'truth' as far as your customers are concerned. |
| | So, before you think about **attracting** customers, what **perception** do you **need to create** in their minds? |
| Positioning | Once you have established the **perceptions** you need to create in the minds of your customers, you then need to **position** everything you do so that you create these desirable perceptions. |
| Suzuki | As you will read later, when Suzuki brought out its four-wheel-drive vehicle it had to think through how it wished to **position** it to create the right **perceptions**. Wrongly positioned, it could have come across as a smaller, cheaper Land Rover. Instead, by brilliant **positioning**, it was established as a cult vehicle in Chelsea and as a fun vehicle to be used in rallies. |
| Positioning Statement | Ideally, you ought to write what is known as a **'Positioning Statement'**, which sets out precisely the way you intend to **position** your product or service to create the required perceptions in the |

minds of your prospective customers that will then make it easier for you to convert them into customers. BMW have been brilliant in the way in which it has positioned its models.

| | |
|---|---|
| Marketing Platform | The way in which you **position** yourself is of crucial importance. It is, in effect, the platform for all your subsequent customer-related activities. |
| Perception Gap | There can often be a gap between the way in which you **are perceived** by your customers and the way in which you would like to **be perceived**. Much of the money you spend on promoting your service or product can be wasted if you are saying one thing when your customers believe another. |

It is therefore vital to monitor regularly the way in which your customers perceive you and your competitors.

If you are selling to a local authority, you may have to influence the appropriate committee. If you are selling to a large organisation, then – though you may talk to the works manager – the decision will be influenced by the financial executive, and confirmed by the chief executive. So, like Nilfisk, you will need to devise a promotion aimed at these decision-makers, as we will see on page 164.

| | |
|---|---|
| Relevant Promotions | The **position** you need for your product or service should influence everything you do to attract customers or clients, as we shall discuss later. |

Case Study        Let us consider one aspect of **positioning** with a case study very
                  kindly written by Ian Catford, Marketing Director of Suzuki GB
                  Cars.

---

## IAN CATFORD ON SUZUKI

Selection and     The marketing of the Suzuki SJ range is a perfect example of the
Creation          **selection** of a **customer segment**, where a product can be positioned
                  and promoted to **create** a particular **customer need** or **demand**.

Positioning       From the Suzuki launch of
                  4 × 4 models in the UK the
                  company has adopted a
                  single-minded approach to
                  its product **positioning**.
                  Instead of introducing the
                  early 4 × 4 LJ80 models into
                  the existing utility market
                  sector, which at that time
                  was dominated by the Land
                  Rover, a decision was taken
                  to **position** the Suzuki as a
                  new leisure activity. It was
                  promoted in a young and
                  aggressive manner as
                  portrayed in the 'Wild
                  Weekender' advertising
                  campaign majoring on the
                  life-style and imagery of
                  owning one of these vehicles
                  and heavily promoting the
                  vehicle as the alternative to
                  the conventional family
                  transport and the ideal
                  second car.

| | |
|---|---|
| Over-all Positioning | Against growing competition in the 4 × 4 market, particularly from increasing numbers of standard saloons offering four-wheel drive option, Suzuki SJ410 has consistently been **positioned** as being a range of true, purpose-built vehicles from the world leaders in lightweight four-wheel drive. |

The importance of getting the **positioning** right is emphasised by the way in which this then becomes the basis on which all subsequent steps to **attract customers** can be taken. Thus, within the over-all **positioning** of Suzuki, specific campaigns have placed emphasis on different aspects of the vehicle.

| | |
|---|---|
| Winter (Hard Top) | 'The Suzuki will keep you mobile even in very adverse weather conditions, making it a practical and affordable – as well as stylish – alternative to a small/ medium saloon car.' |
| Summer (Hard Top and Soft Top) | 'The stylish SJ410 will add zest to your outdoor leisure activities by enabling you to ''get away from it all'' and go where others daren't.' The **positioning** always makes it clear that SJ410, with two-wheel drive option, is also a practical town vehicle. |

POPPING DOWN THE BANK

| | |
|---|---|
| Suzuki Santa | The two Suzuki Santa SJ410s are **positioned** as delivering all the inherent benefits of SJ410 motoring, but with a new, high level of interior comfort and equipment as well as the stylish, fashionable exterior appearance to be expected from the flagships of the range. |

## PERCEPTION

| | |
|---|---|
| Contact Monitoring | To ensure that the Suzuki proposition and presentation of the product met with the belief of the **customer**, continued market research was necessary to monitor the changing attitudes of Suzuki owners. It was very necessary to identify this **customer profile** to ensure that the advertising message and media strategy were on target. |

# ATTRACTING CUSTOMERS

Advertising — Consequently Suzuki's advertising as a result of this changing **user profile** and with the introduction of the higher specification and bigger engined SJ models has, over the last 4–5 years, moved from the 'Wild Weekender' through to the more stylish 'Popping Down the Bank' and 'Shooting Party' colour advertising campaigns. This type of advertising, featured in *Country Life*, *Shooting Times*, *Field*, *Harpers and Queen* etc, has a strong fashion following and appeals to a certain type of Suzuki customer, who are today collectively called the Yuppies or Sloane Rangers.

Adding Value — The total customer orientation is reflected by the research which identified that very few owners had four-wheel driving experience and even fewer had practical experience in driving their vehicles off normal roads. Thus, we **'added value'** by producing a video and handbook on basic Off Road Driving Technique to ensure that the customers could derive maximum value from the product they had purchased.

# RETAINING CUSTOMERS

Owners' Club — We run an owners' club which produces its own magazine and organises not only regional but international cross-country driving competitions. In this way we seek not only to ensure that customers derive the maximum **satisfaction** from their ownership of our vehicles, but also that we create a feeling of 'belonging' which will encourage customer **retention**.

We have teamed up with the National Federation of Zoos in a big drive to help the Black Rhino from extinction in Kenya, and this is very much kept to the fore in our magazine, as shown by the photo of one of the page spreads.

# COMMENTARY

Let us study how Ian's article reflects our Ten Step Plan:

| | |
|---|---|
| **Step One:** Vision | His company does have a clear vision of distributing vehicles to meet customer needs within a socially aware environment. |
| **Steps Two, Three, and Four** | It has carried out market research, to establish customer needs and beliefs, and researched the changing needs and beliefs of customers. |
| **Step Five:** Select | It has chosen a specific market segment and has worked hard to understand the customers in the segment by building up **'customer profiles'**. |
| **Step Six:** Culture | Teaming up with the National Federation of Zoos in a big drive to help save the Black Rhino from extinction in Kenya reflects the company culture of social awareness and reinforces the attractiveness of the product to existing and potential customers. |
| **Step Seven:** Create | By going for the strategic option of niche segment and then 'adding value' to the way in which it met the needs and beliefs of customers, it has created not only a new market-place for itself, but also a new style of life, a new use of vehicles, a new leisure activity, and a new social environment. |
| **Step Eight:** Attract | Before setting out to attract customers, it has thought through the way in which its vehicles should be positioned in the minds of potential customers, and then has worked hard, by ongoing research, to ensure that customer perceptions relate to this positioning statement. |
| **Step Nine:** Satisfy | It has ensured customer satisfaction by providing videos and handbooks for the driving needed for this particular type of vehicle. And, for those interested, it has created a new social activity with its club, linked to a new leisure activity in the national and international rallies it organises. |
| **Step Ten:** Retain | Bringing owners into a club is one excellent way of retaining contact with them but Suzuki also ensures that it has a regular programme of letters to all purchasers of its vehicles, plus a constant programme of product improvement. |

Thus, it demonstrates our Ten Step Plan brilliantly.

# RE-POSITIONING: CHANGING PERCEPTIONS

**Re-positioning**

Sometimes, particularly as a company grows, it is necessary to **re-position** both the company and its products or services.

I faced this problem. I started as one man with a dog, and a part-time secretary. I called myself Ronald Sewell and Associates. As my business grew, we became involved in working for large public companies and, eventually, international companies. But our name still conveyed the impression of 'one man and a dog'.

We had consciously to **re-position** ourselves more accurately as 'Sewells International'. Woolworths, too, have a re-positioning problem.

**Negative Attitude**

In the early 1980s Babycham was perceived as a young (not adult), unfashionable, out of date brand; particularly among older women and other non-drinkers.

**Re-positioning**

Advertising played a key role in demonstrating that Babycham is appropriate to more social drinking in a modern, adult and stylish way and to give the brand a harder, more assertive and confident edge.

Under the new strategy, an advertising execution was developed which moved away from the well-known animated cartoon format to a modern, live action treatment. This was introduced in Summer 1986 and has been successful in re-positioning Babycham away from its previously young and old-fashioned image. This has had the effect of converting increased awareness and interest in Babycham into a growth in consumer purchases in both the On and Off Trade sectors. This trend was further encouraged by the development of new packaging formats (75cl bottle, 25cl cans) and updated packaging designs. In addition, the brand was able to respond to much more aggressive on-pack consumer promotional devices. This strategy stimulated growth at a time when other speciality drinks showed little or no growth.

# TO INFLUENCE 'THIRD PARTY' CUSTOMERS

Third Party
Customers

At the very basic level, if you are selling a product or service to a husband, you may need to ensure that you gain the sympathetic understanding of the wife. If you are selling to a business, you need to ensure that the financial executive and chief executive are likely to approve the order you secure from one of their subordinates.

Influence
the Decision

The question of **positioning** can be even more important if you rely on a third party to make, or to influence, the decision to buy your product or service.

For example, if you are making and selling roofing tiles, it is likely that they will be specified by an architect even though his client is paying the bill. So you will need to devise a promotion campaign for architects.

Creating
Awareness

This was the problem facing Nilfisk, the world's largest manufacturer of industrial suction cleaners. Because of the quality of its product, it was able to interest the executive in charge of cleaning but the people who had to sign the cheque had never heard of Nilfisk.

Its advertising agency, Foster Seligman Wright of Norwich, had to create awareness among these more senior business executives, who were unlikely to read trade papers relating to industrial cleaning. *(Industrial Marketing Digest.)*

National Media

The problem was how to create a **marketing platform or position** when conventional advertising in the national media likely to be read by business executives could be expensive; particularly when it was still necessary to run lead-producing advertisements in the trade and technical press.

Pocket
Cartoons

Pocket cartoons are a clever solution. Since Osbert Lancaster, no one has demanded that cartoons be large. Moreover, cartoons tend to attract attention. So, a trial run of cartoons was placed in the *Sunday Times* and *Financial Times*. These early ads simply had the cartoon, the Nilfisk name and logo, and the slogan 'The World's largest manufacturers of Industrial Suction Cleaners'.

Eventually more national newspapers were used and a regular programme of twelve cartoons a year has been commissioned, primarily from Larry.

| Awareness Improved | Investment in awareness advertising worked and Nilfisk is now well known to business executives. |
|---|---|

**Awareness Improved** — Investment in awareness advertising worked and Nilfisk is now well known to business executives.

**Reaching Supervisors** — While the initial ads were placed in the more serious newspapers likely to be read by senior business executives, the same campaign was extended into the daily newspapers likely to be read by factory managers and supervisors.

**Positioning 'Window'** — We are all bombarded with thousands of advertising messages every day. The Nilfisk campaign is a brilliant example of creating a 'window' in the consciousness of the executives whose organisations are likely to be customers. In short, it is a fine example of creating a **marketing platform** by very clever **positioning**.

# STEP EIGHT: PERCEPTIONS

## CREATING THE RIGHT PERCEPTIONS

Problem

While most of us have a sympathetic desire to help a small, newly started company, we have to protect the interests of our own company. Does a small company have the depth and breadth of experience we need? Is it financially secure? Will it survive and thus be able to provide continuity of service? In the late 1970s these concerns applied particularly to the rash of new software companies which were then starting. Most of them were preoccupied with the technology of what they were doing and demonstrated all the classic symptoms of being '**product-led**'.

Solution

The directors of one computer software company, Engineering Computer Services, decided to be **market-driven**. They made the conscious decision to invest heavily in promotions to create the **perceptions** they needed potential clients to have. *(Industrial Marketing Digest.)*

Investing in Promotions

In fact, in the first few years of its existence – the firm started in 1975 – they regularly invested between 15 per cent and 20 per cent of turnover in promotion. As a result, they created a **perception** that ECS was a very much larger and longer established company than it was in fact.

'Established' Image

ECS spent £20,000 on its exhibit at the 1982 Engineering Design Show (which was equivalent to £2,000 for every member on the then payroll) to project an 'established' image.

A Strong Company

Its disproportionate early expenditure on advertising and exhibitions paid off. When its sales executive followed up leads, he was seldom challenged on the size of the company, or the number of installations. The enquirer already had the **perception** that Engineering Computer Services was a strong company which was going to be around for a long time.

Attention to Detail

This **positioning** was reinforced by attention to detail. This included 'paying over-the-odds' for people; using engineers to sell to engineers and providing their engineers with quality cars.

| | |
|---|---|
| Confidence Factors | In fact, everything ECS does is designed to create the **perception** it wished in the minds of customers, down to high quality stationery and literature. |

## 'MERE PERCEPTION'

| | |
|---|---|
| 'We're OK, it's only a Perception Problem' | *A Passion for Excellence* is well worth reading on the subject of 'mere perception'. Author Tom Peters had been reviewing some of the problems within a large capital-goods manufacturer. Invariably, the response of the engineers was that 'We're OK, it's only a perception problem'. But, as he points out, the real problem is that **perception** is all there is. There is no reality. Perception is truth to the perceiver. |
| | It is the perceptions that we create, or fail to create, in the minds of our customers that determine whether our business is successful, or an 'also ran'. |
| Define | Can you define the **perceptions** you **need** to create in the minds of your customers **before** they make the decision on whether or not to buy from you? |
| | Do you have a conscious programme for making sure that you create the desired **perceptions**? |
| Discover | Do you consciously set out to discover the **actual perceptions** your existing and potential customers have about you and your organisation, your products, and services? |
| | Seeing ourselves as others see us is always difficult. But in business it is vital. |
| | It may well be that we need to ask our advertising agency or some independent person to carry out an exercise to determine how we are perceived, so that we can close any '**gap**' which has opened up. |

## PERCEPTION STUDY QUESTIONNAIRE

Interviewer number  _____     Location  _____

*Spontaneous Recall*

A. NEW

1.  Can you tell me the name of a garage specialising in the sale of new cars?
_____
2.  Who's cars do they sell? _____
3.  Do you know their location? (give address) _____
4.  How would you rate their reputation? (Circle answer)
    Very Bad            Poor              Mediocre              Good              Excellent
5.  Is this garage a member of any trade association?     YES / NO / DON'T KNOW
    If 'YES' do you know which one? (please specify) _____
_____


B. USED

1.  Can you tell me the name of a garage specialising in the sale of used cars?
_____
2.  Do you know their location? (give address) _____
3.  How would you rate their reputation? (circle answer)
    Very Bad            Poor              Mediocre              Good              Excellent
4.  Is this garage a member of any trade association?     YES / NO / DON'T KNOW
    If 'YES' do you know which one? (please specify) _____
_____


C. SERVICE/REPAIR

1.  Can you tell me the name of a garage specialising in vehicle servicing/repair?
_____
2.  Do you know their location? (give address) _____
3.  How would you rate their reputation? (circle answer)
    Very Bad            Poor              Mediocre              Good              Excellent
4.  Is this garage a member of any trade association?     YES / NO / DON'T KNOW
    If 'YES' do you know which one? (please specify)_____
_____


*Prompted Recall*

1.  Have you heard of ABC garage?     YES / NO   If 'NO' — end questionnaire
2.  Do you know their location? (give address) _____
3.  How would you rate their reputation? (circle answer)

| NEW | Very Bad | Poor | Mediocre | Good | Excellent |
|---|---|---|---|---|---|
| USED | Very Bad | Poor | Mediocre | Good | Excellent |
| SERVICE/REPAIR | Very Bad | Poor | Mediocre | Good | Excellent |

*Personal*

1.  What make of car do you drive?_____
2.  When did you last visit a garage to buy a new or used car or to have your car serviced or repaired?
    (circle answer)
               0–2 months                3–9 months                over 9 months

# STEP EIGHT: PROMOTING YOUR PRODUCT OR SERVICE

## 'PERSPIRATION NOT INSPIRATION'

Test and
Measure

When we first start in business, we are not sure what is going to be the best method of promoting ourselves. If we follow our competitors, it may be a question of the 'the blind leading the blind'.

The only answer is to **test and measure** so that we can gradually build up hard evidence of what works and what does not work. Every time you spend money on a promotion, be it an advert or a direct mail campaign, head up a sheet of paper, enter how much the promotion costs you and try to record how much business resulted.

It never ceases to amaze me that companies can spend vast sums of money on various promotions, and yet not have a detailed analysis of how much it costs them, and the benefits they gained as a result.

Evaluation
Panels

If a particular promotion was not cost-effective, was it because you used the wrong media, or because you failed to put across the right message?

It can be useful to form a small 'evaluation panel' from business colleagues (perhaps friends from Round Table or Rotary) and ask them for their reactions to your advert or direct mail message, or your leaflet. If they had been customers for your product or service, would they have been enthused to buy? If not, why not?

You may be an instinctive copywriter and have a flair for design, or you may have to work hard to learn by experience, but you won't benefit from experience unless you seek constructive criticisms from existing or potential customers.

Priority Task

In small, and even not so small, companies, **product-led** executives naturally tend to be preoccupied with what they are **doing**.

In **cost-constrained** companies, there is a fear of spending too much on money promotions.

In **sales-driven** companies, the emphasis is not so much on **investing** but in **throwing** the money at the problem in terms of discounts, and other price-reduction gimmicks.

In a **customer-driven** company, the emphasis is on making a deliberate long-term **investment** to create the **perceptions** needed to gain business from previously identified customers.

Options

Building up turnover is not a matter of inspiration, but perspiration. It requires 'hard slogging' effort to concentrate on finding the most cost-effective ways of attracting the volume of business you need.

To help, you will find below (starting on p. 170) an alphabetical list of some of the options open to you when you set about attracting your customers.

Persistence

Obviously, I do not have the time to help you with a detailed explanation about how to implement every technique mentioned later. But some techniques need a consistent approach.

It is well known that advertisers tend to get fed up with their adverts at about the time that their customers begin to take notice of them!

Sending one direct-mail letter by itself may be a total waste of money. You may need to plan a campaign of two or three or even five or six direct-mail letters to achieve the result you require.

The *Industrial Marketing Digest* contains some extremely interesting case studies on these and related points.

Organisation

If we agree the objective is to identify, attract, satisfy, and retain customers, then we need to create an organisation in which somebody has the specific responsibility for **attracting** customers. If you are starting a company, then you ought to take charge – like Anita Roddick – of **attracting** customers.

As you grow, you may need to recruit an appropriately qualified executive to take over this role. But don't just over-promote a salesman. The process of **attracting** customers is more than mere face-to-face selling. It embraces everything that your company does, and thus needs someone able to implement every aspect of identifying, attracting, satisfying, and retaining customers.

Good Selling is
Good Serving

People want to buy. Individuals enjoy shopping. Businesses will not succeed unless people can buy the products and the services they need.

So, you and your business need to create an environment within which you become eager to offer your customers the opportunity to buy. If you have designed a product or service which truly meets customers' needs, then if they say no it can only be the way in which you approach them!

| | |
|---|---|
| Promotions: Objectives | Before placing any form of advertising or promotion, it is advisable to go back to our Ten Step Success Plan: |

- Will it reflect your vision?

- Is it related to a thorough understanding of the market-place?

- Will it reflect the benefits that customers are seeking?

- Will it have regard to the way in which customers are sub-divided into segments?

- Will it address itself to the specific groups of customers or segments you have chosen as your target in the language they will appreciate?

- Will it explain your mission?

- Will it reflect 'added values' and other benefits you are seeking to create in your product or service?

- Will it create the right perception to reinforce your position?

- Does it build on the strengths of your particular company and its products or services?

## IDEAS FOR ATTRACTING CUSTOMERS

| | |
|---|---|
| Accessibility | If attracting customers depends on getting them to inspect your products, than **accessibility** becomes very important. The Body Shop ensures that its products are accessible by the way they can be looked at, have the signs read, the testers tested, the soaps smelled, the lotions dipped into, the herbal ingredients pondered, and the perfume bar sniffed at and mused over. |
| Advertising | If you decide to advertise, the media in which you can do so is enormous, as indicated below: |

Cinemas

Consumer magazines and periodicals

Directories, including Yellow Pages

'Free issue papers'

Local press

National press

Regional press

Sunday press

Trade, technical, and professional publications

Radio

TV

In addition you can use posters on buses, taxis, parking meters, and other places to display your message.

Obviously, the choice of media to use is very much a function of your previous analysis of the specific segment you are striving to reach. The fact that your local regional newspaper has a circulation of 500,000 is irrelevant. How many of those readers are in the market segments you are seeking to attract?

## BASIC AD. CHECKLIST...

### Minimum standards every ad should meet

*Check your proposition for maximum appeal*

**Yes No**

- [ ] [ ] Proposition clear, easily grasped?
- [ ] [ ] Item or event right for your target audience?
- [ ] [ ] Excellent value on popular merchandise?

**Yes No**

- [ ] [ ] All possible name appeal?
- [ ] [ ] Would additional items expand appeal?

### Check your headline for attention value

- [ ] [ ] Best selling idea in headline?
- [ ] [ ] **Use of five great proven headline ingredients?**
- [ ] [ ] (1) Promise benefits.
- [ ] [ ] (2) Use of "new" or "news".
- [ ] [ ] (3) Mention prospect and/or prospect's interest.
- [ ] [ ] (4) Favourable product mention.
- [ ] [ ] (5) Pertinent appeal to curiosity.

### Check your body copy for interest and persuasion

- [ ] [ ] Immediately enlarges on headline promise?
- [ ] [ ] Benefits clearly presented?
- [ ] [ ] Benefits supported by product points?
- [ ] [ ] Exclusive and only features presented?
- [ ] [ ] Popularity claimed and demonstrated?
- [ ] [ ] Confidence built with assurances, proof?
- [ ] [ ] Value conveyed positively, definitely?
- [ ] [ ] Excuses, reasons for buying included?
- [ ] [ ] Choosing, buying made easy?
- [ ] [ ] Sell for your store alone?
- [ ] [ ] Bid for action?
- [ ] [ ] Headline idea repeated at least twice?
- [ ] [ ] All questions and objections answered?
- [ ] [ ] All vital facts included?
- [ ] [ ] Language simple, uncomplicated?
- [ ] [ ] Honest, factual, service-rendering?
- [ ] [ ] If read to a prospect would it sell him/her?
- [ ] [ ] Credit, other services included?

### Check your layout and art for clear communication

- [ ] [ ] Illustration attracts favourable attention?
- [ ] [ ] Illustration aids perception?
- [ ] [ ] Logos top and bottom?
- [ ] [ ] Layout simple, uncluttered?
- [ ] [ ] Elements in logical sequence?
- [ ] [ ] Simple borders, type styles?
- [ ] [ ] No type over pictures or tints?
- [ ] [ ] Body copy set in caps and lower case?
- [ ] [ ] Type large enough?
- [ ] [ ] Type columns not too wide or narrow?
- [ ] [ ] Body copy all black and white?
- [ ] [ ] No body copy set in caps or italics?
- [ ] [ ] Long copy broken with crossheads?
- [ ] [ ] Entire ad easy and inviting to read?
- [ ] [ ] Headline, subheads, illustrations tell story?
- [ ] [ ] In character with your dealership?

Advertising
Advice

If your customers need advice, then your adverts could feature a 'tip of the week' as a way of encouraging your customers to come to your resident expert for more detailed and personal advice.

Advertising:
Business

Years ago, McGraw-Hill Business Publications ran a classic advertisement which we are grateful for permission to reproduce:

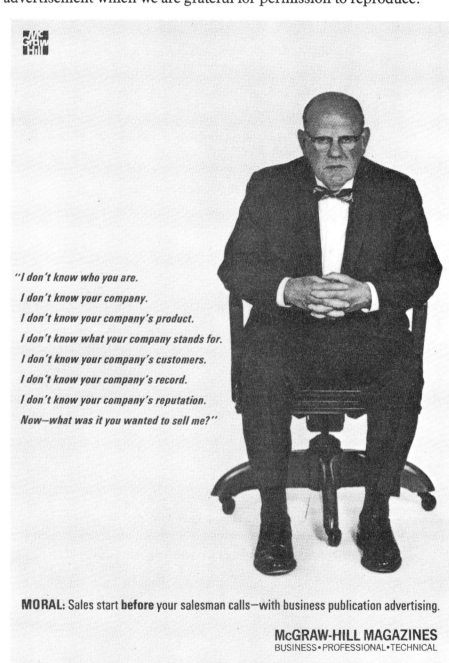

"I don't know who you are.
I don't know your company.
I don't know your company's product.
I don't know what your company stands for.
I don't know your company's customers.
I don't know your company's record.
I don't know your company's reputation.
Now—what was it you wanted to sell me?"

**MORAL:** Sales start **before** your salesman calls—with business publication advertising.

**McGRAW-HILL MAGAZINES**
BUSINESS•PROFESSIONAL•TECHNICAL

Clearly, as business publishers they have a vested interest in business advertising. Yet, even companies who spend heavily on direct marketing techniques recognise the value of business advertising. As we saw with Nilfisk, it creates awareness among both those who buy and those who may be involved in the purchase decision. As we saw with Engineering Computer Services, it can also create a climate of confidence.

**Advertising: Classified**

Classified advertisements are normally regarded as a method of selling low-value products with very little creativity being employed.

ABERTAY, a small company marketing paper sacks to farmers, has used a campaign of classified advertisements with such good effect that it became a dominant supplier. At first, they featured a pretty girl; and secondly, to gain reader involvement, a competition for slogans and for limericks. This enabled a different limerick or verse to be used each week and provided the winning entrants with the satisfaction of seeing their names in print and a modest prize. *(Industrial Marketing Digest.)*

Uniquely, the advertising campaign caught on with the entire agricultural community, whether farmers, their wives, or merchants, with every sector of the community taking an interest.

However, the regular campaign in the farming press was achieved with a 3-inch, single-column advertisement where the formula, the girls, and the jokes shared by the market-place gave the ads a display-type impact at the cost of a small classified advertisement.

Such a campaign would only work in a situation where, like Jim Sutherland, the owner of Abertay, you are prepared to devote a great deal of personal effort to sustain the campaign and to enforce its friendly impact with an equally friendly service.

**Advertising:
Comparative**

It does not always pay to run adverts where you compare your own product or service with its principal competitors, particularly where you appear to be knocking your competitors. Often some of this competitive advertising provides welcome publicity to your competitors at your expense.

**Advertising:
Corporate**

*Goodbye to the low profile* (Mercury Books) describes how Mobil ran a corporate advertising campaign in the US to change an adverse public impression of the oil industry that existed there during the 1970s.

In South Devon Trago Mills run full-page ads commenting – forcefully – on local issues. But such 'corporate' advertising needs to be handled carefully.

**After-sales
Service**

If you are selling a major item of equipment, or even a minor item such as a lawnmower, washing machine, or other item of kitchen equipment, then the after-sales service you provide can be promoted as an attraction to your customers.

**Ambience**

The ambience you create within your business is important to the customers you seek to attract. Tim Waterstone started a new career at the age of 42. He now has a national chain of 18 bookshops, which has contributed to a quiet revolution in the way books are sold.

'What we have done is moved away from the traditional bookshop image and tried to create a **theatre-like** atmosphere where people can wander round and have a thoroughly good time,' Mr Waterstone explains.

The shops offer a wide range of titles, well kept by the staff who understand and care about literature.

Similarly, the Pentos Group has spent £2m on its Dillons the Bookstore in Gower Street. Sales have gone up from £7m to £11.5m in a year!

**Annual Accounts and Reports**

Your annual accounts can be used positively as a means of influencing and even attracting customers, and 'third parties' like the press.

For years Brian Allison of Business Intelligence Services sent me his well illustrated and interestingly written annual accounts.

Some larger organisations now produce three separate documents, one for statutory purposes, one for employees, and one for customers and PR purposes.

| | |
|---|---|
| Appointment Selling | The technique of gaining an appointment to see a customer at work, or at home, to present your product or service. The appointment is normally obtained by phoning the potential customer, his secretary or wife, to ask for the appointment. Or customers might be encouraged to respond to an advert or direct-mail letter, whereupon the suggestion of a meeting can be put forward. |
| Articles | Progressive organisations recognise the value of 'placing' articles in appropriate national, trade, or technical publications. This is a two-way trade. The magazine is glad to receive an authoritative contribution. The organisation gains kudos as being perceived to be an expert in its field.

You may be lucky in having an executive able to write interesting articles. If not, your PR company may be able to write such an article on behalf of, and in collaboration with, one of your own executives. |
| Audio Cassettes | How do you reach customers in a distinctive way? One solution is to send them an audio cassette. Given the high standards we have been trained to expect from radio announcers, the quality of voice reproduction will need to be first-class. To create the right **perceptions**, the quality of the printing on the cassette itself and on its container will need to be good.

The dialogue should convey your message, in an interesting and amusing manner. Cost will depend on the number produced, but could range between 50p and £1.00 a cassette, though what matters of course is the 'cost per response'. This might work out at between £5.00 and £10.00 per customer. IMD had a case study on this in one issue. |
| Birthday Cards | Birthday and other anniversary cards can be a useful way of keeping in contact with your customers. Our own company is well known for the care we take to find and reproduce a poem which aptly expresses the value of Christmas. |
| Books: Product Launches, Company Histories | Long-established companies will often commission a lavishly illustrated book on their history, probably a justified indulgence on the part of the company concerned.

Greater impact can be achieved when the book is written about a particularly successful product. Thus, Edouard Siedler's on the launch of the Ford Fiesta helped generate interest and enthusiasm for the product. |

| | |
|---|---|
| Books: Sponsors | The company-sponsored book has been used in America for over 30 years and is beginning to become recognised in the UK. For example, *Protect Yourself* is a complete guide to safeguarding your home by Master Lock. Another, *The Hyperactive Child*, was sponsored by the drug company Smith Kline. The American reader absorbs the message without fully realising it is part of a wider marketing campaign. In Britain, examples are the *Guinness Book of Records* or *Michelin Maps*. |

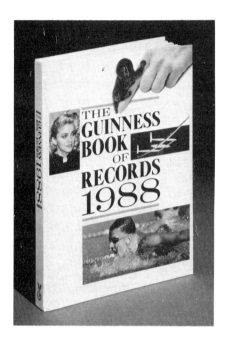

On a more practical level, Herring Son and Daw, a leading firm of chartered surveyors with a specialised motor trade property section, produced a major report on the future of the motor trade and its impact on property values. In this way it demonstrated its expertise and commitment to its customers in the trade.

| | |
|---|---|
| Boxes | The boxes in which you sell your products can be an important aid to attracting customers, particularly if your products reach the customer through any form of self-service outlets. Study the shelves as you shop. |
| Brochures | A good, well presented brochure about your company is a vital aid in creating a 'marketing platform' to **position** your company correctly, and may also achieve direct sales. |

| | |
|---|---|
| Cable TV | By far the most promising medium for home-shopping, if the experience of the US is anything to go by, is cable TV. |
| | Swindon has mounted a home-shopping programme with BT and Littlewoods. Other cable stations at Westminster and Milton Keynes have been operating text-based shopping services. |
| | Every child from now on will be educated to think of interacting with a TV as second nature. |
| Calendars | An annual calendar which an existing or potential customer sees every day of the year can be a cost-effective advertising medium. However, they have to be attractive. |
| Canvassing | On our own training courses, we have got salesmen to walk up one side of the High Street and back down the other, calling into every business with a few friendly words of greeting, and leaving a visiting card. Invariably the shop-keepers are very pleased that somebody has taken the time to call on them and thus it generates goodwill, and, in many instances, actual sales have resulted. |
| Carrier Bags | We all recognise someone who has been shopping at M & S or Hamleys – by their carrier bags. |

| | |
|---|---|
| Catalogues | For many organisations, producing a catalogue is a cost-centre. Habitat has long sold its catalogue as an aid to shopping. Indeed many shoppers use it as a pre-shopping guide. |

| Catalogue Shopping | Analysing sales normally shows that 80 per cent of sales are achieved from 20 per cent of stock items, though slower-moving items provide an essential element of the service you provide to customers. | |

OYA Design unit to show off Homebase services

Sainsbury's Homebase has come up with a means of promoting an extended product inventory, with a 'shop within a shop' called 'Homebase Extra Service'. With representative product samples on display, customers can choose from six different catalogues and order more specialised items than might be on offer in the store itself.

| Celebrations | As individuals we like to celebrate; similarly, business organisations can justifiably celebrate a successful event: the gaining of an order or contract, the extension of a factory, or another success story.

It can motivate the executives and employees of the company concerned. It can generate news stories in the media which will enhance the company in the eyes of customers, potential customers, suppliers, and sources of finance!

You can include your customers by inviting them to a reception, an open day, a dinner, or by sending them some celebration gift to cement your relationship with them further. |

| Conferences or Seminars | A conference or seminar can be a useful way of generating the goodwill of customers, or the goodwill of those best able to influence your customers. Moreover, organising a conference may help to **position** you as an organisation prepared to serve your particular trade or industry by creating a forum at which to discuss areas of concern.

Thus, a company called TAC organised a conference of architects to debate their reaction to the developments likely to be needed in the market for man-made slates. Not only did this conference gain significant PR exposure in the magazine for professional architects, it also gave them invaluable advice which they were able to incorporate into the 'marketing platform' from which they subsequently gained market leadership. *(Industrial Marketing Digest.)* |

# MARKETING THE VBRA AND ITS MEMBERS

The VBRA (Vehicle Builders and Repairers Association) embarked upon its new marketing initiative to tackle the adverse and low key image of the trade.

The first stage, the Premier Bodyshop Programme, helped members to understand the benefits of giving premises a face-lift, providing new reception areas and of having staff and company vehicles presented in the appropriate livery.

The aim was to provide a new image of VBRA members to the public and the first stage proved so successful that the range of services offered to members was extended to include items of stationery bearing the association's logo.

The success of those members who took part provided the incentive to the sceptical. The initiative gained momentum. High profile leaflets with a retention value were issued by members to the public outlining procedures to adopt after an accident and explaining the work of the 'Bodyshop'.

So successful was the initiative that the VBRA now has a separate limited company which operates a service to members for the sale of marketing aids.

Corporate Image

Whenever a small company seeks the advice of a local advertising studio, they are told that they need to improve their corporate image. This results in a proposal for a new 'logo'. This is an ineffective waste of money. A logo – by itself – has no impact; particularly if it is changed every time a new agency comes along!

But it is very important to create a corporate image which creates the right perception in the minds of existing or prospective customers. This needs to be reflected in a 'house style', if not some form of corporate branding.

Lovell Construction created a new corporate image with the now familiar green on yellow Lovell 'L', the sloping parallel bars of which managed to combine the ideas of both strength and movement.

This corporate image was painted at the entrance to every site on which it was working. This helped to stress both the number and widespread location of the sites on which it had contracts. You may also have seen this logo on the side of London taxis.

However, it was but one aspect of a very strong 'personality' created for Lovells. Other aspects included innovative use of videos which demonstrated some of the projects it had handled; the creation of a slogan 'Look at Lovells' and a series of strong advertisements featuring 'Lovell's Law', all based on a strong commitment to, and involvement of, the executives and employees of all the companies within the group.

**Competitions**

It is possible to attract customers by competitions which make them aware of your products and services and, ideally, make them aware of your location, your products, services, and staff.

A basic example is organising a painting competition in liaison with local schools.

If you sell lawnmowers, you can sponsor a lawnmower race. If you sell more advanced equipment, you can sponsor a 'technician of the year' competition on your equipment.

**Counter Selling**

The prime technique in most shops and other organisations dealing directly with customers, such as travel agents. Good selection and training of staff is essential.

**Counter Units**

The counter units from which your parts are sold by yourself, or by one of your retailers, can be a key element in achieving a sale.

A company called Tuckers, which markets fixing bolts called Parabolts for builders, built a special counter unit with photographs of its product and cut-outs featuring the bolts used in a difficult situation, stressing their benefits. *(Industrial Marketing Digest.)*

In addition, the back of the unit displays a chart of easy sales points and the equivalent Parabolts parts' numbers of competitors' products. This information not only gave the salesman the confidence to sell benefits, but also enabled him to sell Parabolts in place of competitors' products.

**Credit Terms**

As David Alliance found, granting credit is an excellent way of gaining customers.

Stores such as Marks & Spencer have their own credit card. This has not only generated the profit on the finance but a marvellous database of customers should M & S decide to go into direct-mail marketing.

As you may know, some tailors and other stores run a 'budget account', so that if the customer pays, say, £30 a month he can buy goods to the value of £360.

Many businesses now make more money from the provision of credit than from the goods themselves!

Customer
Clubs

One way of 'adding value' is to make sure that your customers derive the maximum possible benefit from the product or service they buy from you. One way of doing this is to create a 'customer club'.

The Grundfos Pumps Better Business Club is described in a contribution by Nevill Wade of Welbeck P.R.

---

## GRUNDFOS PUMPS BETTER BUSINESS CLUB

Since the rapid growth of the central heating market, there have been few attempts to provide technical and business information for use by an increasing number of installers, many of whom own their own small firms. Grundfos Pumps Better Business Club is one approach to improving this situation.

As a result of this rise in demand, a large number of installers set up in business and it became evident from questions asked of Grundfos by them, that there was a lack of information about specialised subjects of commercial benefit. Other requests made to the company had indicated a need for technical information on pumps – a key part of any central-heating system. Grundfos, who wanted to forge closer links with installers, responded by forming the Better Business Club to provide installers with facts about relevant business topics and technical matters. The Club's aim is to save time for installers, providing at-a-glance reference material on subjects of professional interest, in a format difficult to obtain elsewhere.

Details on business issues are forwarded to club members in the form of Circulation File Sheets – these have covered subjects such as profit improvement, investment, business vehicles, pensions and advertising. The information is provided in a clear succinct format for easy reference. Circulation file sheets are complemented by Technical File Sheets, written because Grundfos had discovered that readily available technical information for installers, not biased in favour of a particular system or manufacturer, was virtually non-existent. The Technical File Sheets create an easily acceptable library of relevant data on subjects ranging from pump maintenance to system trouble shooting.

Membership of the Better Business Club, prompted on reply cards inserted into Grundfos Pumps' point of sale packaging, continues to expand, as does the range of benefits and materials available to those members. In 1986, a questionnaire was distributed, requesting suggestions for new forms of activity, and asking for opinions on the usefulness of the club. As a result of the findings, a binder was designed so that various information sheets can be quickly referred to, and additional information about Grundfos in the form of exhibition invitations and news bulletins is now included in the mailings when appropriate. Additionally, a number of special offers relating to microcomputing, tools and installation equipment are being planned.

Other measures are continually being evaluated and introduced for the benefit of Better Business Club members. 'Pump Talk', Grundfos company newspaper, produced by Welbeck Public Relations, is enclosed in two of the quarterly mailings, providing news about products and installation.

The 'Operation Update' series was produced in response to requests from installers asking for information on a large installation that took advantage of recent technical developments in all aspects of the heating industry. 'Operation Update', in all three parts, covers faults in an old central-heating system, details how a new efficient system was substituted, and gives the installer's view of the project, including his ideas about winning business.

In addition, the Better Business Club has also devised a series of seminars designed to provide practical and concrete advice for installers aiming to expand their businesses. The seminars, a day in duration, take the form of Grundfos personnel and consultants offering advice and information on such techniques as business management, advertising and public relations.

The Better Business Club has now been operational for 3½ years, and both Grundfos and club members believe that it provides a useful service. Because of the demand for extra information and facilities, BBC mailings have been increased from two to four a year. Membership, denoted by a personal indentification card, is expected to increase again as more installers become aware of what the club can offer.

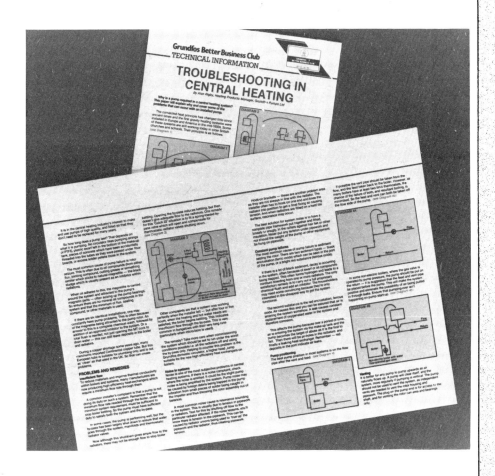

| | |
|---|---|
| Customer Database | When we were discussing the importance of systems in Step Seven, we discussed the importance of building up a complete database relating not only to current customers, but lapsed customers, and every potential customer with whom your business has had contact. Thus, even a lost customer who decided not to buy from you should be on your system so that you have a chance of 'converting' him when he re-enters the market for your product or service. |
| | One reason for building up this database is to be able to have a programme of '**constant customer communication**'. |
| | If you have not yet built this essential database, then you need to do so as quickly as possible. (See the Direct Response story on page 209.) |
| Customer Panels | After asking customers for their views on how you can better meet their needs, is not only common sense, but can be a way of building very close customer relations. |
| | A company making man-made roofing slates retained two architects to advise them on how to produce brochures and other aids which would make life easier for architects to specify their particular slates. Anything you can do to learn more how to meet the needs of your customers or those – like architects – in a position to influence their decision must be worthwhile. |
| Customer Questionnaires | Persuading your customer or client to fill in a questionnaire can be a valuable form of research. In Step Two we discussed the way in which commercial research companies gain invaluable information about the life-styles of customers for different products. |
| | If you set out to ask your customers their views, and they sense that you are genuinely seeking to provide a worthwhile service, they will respond favourably. You will get useful advice, build a platform for subsequent successful promotions, and even get some sales leads from the responses. |
| | Toyota gets a 48–49 per cent response rate whenever it asks its private customers to complete such a questionnaire. |
| Dealer/ Distributor Promotions | If you sell your products or services through an intermediary, such as a dealer or distributor, it makes sense to motivate them to sell your product or service. |
| | Thorough training should be regarded as an integrated aspect of all your promotional activities. Volkswagen is spending millions on a |

training programme for every employee of every one of its dealers in Europe from the managing director down to the floorsweeper.

Most organisations selling to dealers or distributors have a programme of incentives which come into operation when they achieve or exceed sales targets.

Deliveries

Nothing is more irritating to customers who go all through the selection process, decide what they want to buy, and then are told they cannot take the item on display but will have to wait three or four weeks, or longer, for delivery.

So prompt delivery, linked with a pleasant hand-over of the item which has been purchased, is a very important element in attracting, satisfying, and retaining customers.

Designing and Planning Services

The new generation of fitted kitchens is a prime example of where upmarket companies justify a premium price by offering a design service linked to the precise dimensions of their customers' kitchen area.

As another example, Dana Brothers of Swindon offer a computerised design service to garages wishing to improve the design, layout, and equipment of their workshops.

Design of Shops, Offices, and Warehouses

Anita Roddick's sense of style was responsible for initiating and maintaining the visual impact of The Body Shop. This includes the green paintwork, rustic woodshelving, potted ferns, and handwritten look of the labels and signs.

Since then she has modified and continually brought up to date all aspects of The Body Shop design with a team of different designers from various companies. She regards it as 'incredibly important' to get people able to create the right image.

Similar principles need to be applied to all areas visited by customers, including professional offices and even workshops. Tom Farmer works hard to give his Kwik-Fit workshops the right image.

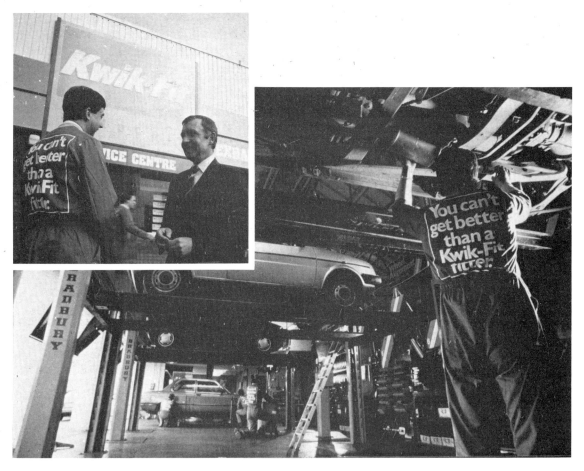

Desk-top Presentations

Computer software is now being developed to enable the production of graphs, bar charts, and pie charts which can be stored on a diskette. These can then be presented on a portable computer.

'Live' presentation will have more dramatic impact on customers and will cost far less than producing videos or slides.

Direct Mail

An engineering firm specialising in stainless steel fabrication decided to send a direct selling letter to the key decision-maker in a wide range of suitable prospective customers. The name of the key decision-maker had been researched by telephone to verify the information contained in a directory such as 'Kompass' which gives the names of local businesses and their executives. *(Industrial Marketing Digest.)*

The direct mail shot was followed up by a telephone call and the company also contacted the previous customers both by letter and phone. The results were very embarrassing as the firm could not cope with the business it had generated – a good deal of which was much more profitable than the work it had in hand.

Sadly, there are too few organisations which really do provide good customer services. It is likely that your prospective customers are waiting for you to demonstrate your ability to meet their needs. Direct mail is one way you can demonstrate your ability to do so.

Direct Response

This is a technique of seeking to sell from the page of an advert by incorporating an order form within the advertisement. You have only to read the colour supplements of the Sunday newspapers to see how widespread this technique has become.

The *Industrial Marketing Digest* once described a firm which advertises domestic furniture in a wide range of magazines to sell on a direct response basis. The name and details of each reply are entered on to a computer database, together with the date on which the enquiry was received. An informative selling pack is sent off immediately.

After an appropriate interval the company telephones each prospect to discuss queries and to attempt to close the sale. The conversion rate is very high and the computer is then used to process orders and monitor delivery.

Those who do not purchase are listed separately and then receive regular follow-up mailings. These consist of a newsletter plus special offers. The promotion – particularly its regularity – is an important means of creating a feeling of security and trust which helps to encourage subsequent purchases. About half the initial non-purchasers do eventually buy.

Once customers buy, they are contacted regularly every three months. They are sent personalised letters offering a wide range of purchasing opportunities: to buy new units, to trade in old units, special discount offers, and interest-free credit.

Finally, customers are encouraged to introduce the products to their friends and relations by incentives such as cash, discounts, prizes, or holidays. As a result, 50 per cent of new orders now come from previous customers and their referrals.

So, the direct response technique is used to build a customer database from which telephone selling and direct-mail marketing can follow.

Display Stands   Attractively presented can be a 'silent salesman' on your behalf.

Electronic Shopping   Mail-order companies were quick to pick up on the potential of Oracle. They found it a cheap and efficient means to keep agents up to date with price changes, special offers, and competitions.

Oracle has also built up a successful holiday and travel classified advertising business. Advertising on Oracle can be cross-referred from TV commercials.

Littlewoods offer their Shop TV catalogue to all users of Prestel who are linked with the mainframe computer.

```
P171   ORACLE 171 Mon 8 Jun ITV 1205 32
                                        8/8
         HOTLINE SAVERS
         SPRING/SUMMER REDUCTIONS
ITEM    CREAM TRS.        JEANS (not 14)
Page    94/B(not 14)      115/G
C.No    EA3096            EA3111
Was     £18.99            £19.99
NOW     £12.99            £14.99
ITEM    CORAL TRS         IVORY JEANS
Page    94/B (16,18)      117/E(14,16,18)
C.No    EA3097            EA3115
Was     £18.99            £17.99
NOW     £12.99            £12.99
ITEM    BLUE TRS.         MINT JEANS
Page    115/F(size 12)    101/G (10,16)
C.No    EA3110            EA3509
Was     £14.99            £14.99
NOW     £ 9.99            £10.99
MORE BARGAINS EVERY MONDAY & THURSDAY
```

**Evening Classes**

Many customers are keen to gain more information. One garage group has run a very successful series of courses for the increasing proportion of women who now buy and maintain their own vehicles.

**Events**

Many companies organise various 'events'. These should be linked to the life-style of the appropriate customers you are seeking to influence.

I have known of companies which organise a bi-monthly evening at the local sports club, a clay pigeon shoot, an opera evening, a golfing day, or take parties to Wimbledon.

While these events are normally used to reinforce relationships with existing customers, they can also be used to invite potential customers.

In the atmosphere of goodwill generated by a successfully organised event, existing satisfied customers will often enthuse about your company to your potential customers, and thus help you both to reinforce your relationship with them, and to open a business relationship with your prospect.

| | |
|---|---|
| Exchanging Goods | Marks & Spencer is a prime example of a company with customer-orientated systems for the prompt exchange of goods.

An undoubted attraction to customers! |
| Exhibitions: Public | There is a publication called 'Exhibitions and Conference Fact Finder' which gives full details of all the exhibitions being held throughout Britain. It is quite amazing to see the number and diversity. |

You then have to decide whether a significantly large number of your customers are likely to visit a particular exhibition to make it worth your while to exhibit.

You cannot rely on the organisers to bring the visitors to the exhibition to your stand. You need to incur the additional cost of a pre-show promotion to bring your prospective customers to see you in preference to your competitors.

You then have to be sure that your staff are trained to handle them correctly. The IMD has a number of illuminating case studies.

| | |
|---|---|
| Exhibitions: Your Own | If you can generate enough material, there is nothing to stop you organising an exhibition of your own, possibly in co-operation with other friendly organisations. IBM has done this, linking its hardware and software with the range of specialist applications. |

| Factory Visits | If you are proud of your company and what it produces, and the team of people that work with you, it can be a marvellous boost to your relationship with your customer or clients to invite them to see your operation. |
|---|---|

Griffiths Laboratory initiated a six-shot direct-mail campaign with the specific objective of getting prospective customers to visit its factory, which it felt was its 'best sales aid'. *(Industrial Marketing Digest.)*

It encouraged prospective customers to send some of their technical people with their marketing and purchasing executives. On arrival these different executives were teamed up with their 'opposite numbers' from Griffiths Laboratory. In this way mutual understanding and confidence were generated.

My wife was once invited to visit the factories where Garibaldi biscuits were made. She came back so impressed with the cleanliness of the operation that she has bought them ever since.

| Free Offers: Mail Shots | When Dow Chemicals wanted to promote a selected weedkiller through a direct-mail campaign to forestry specialists, its free offer (essential for gaining a response to a direct-mail shot) was a guide to the latest techniques in forestry weed control. *(Industrial Marketing Digest.)* |
|---|---|

Doubtless you will have seen or received many 'free offers' for yourself and will be able to judge their effectiveness in persuading you to sample the product and then place an order.

| Freephone 0800 Linklines | Making it easy for potential customers to phone you is common sense. Customers for the Autoglass Windscreen replacement service find their calls answered in 15 seconds, a factor which has helped Autoglass to increases sales by 30%. |
|---|---|

| Freepost | Likewise, Freepost can encourage replies though direct mail specialists say it has more impact to stick an 18p stamp on the reply card you send to customers. |
|---|---|

| Folders | Many customers who are shopping around before making their purchase end up with an untidy collection of leaflets from the businesses they have visited in their research. They often also end up forgetting which salesman they saw at which business. |
|---|---|

It is important to make sure that they do not forget their visit to you. Make sure that all the leaflets you give to them are properly presented in a folder. Ideally these folders should have a photograph of your sales person (your business and product) so they can recall the person who served them.

Graphic Design

Sales of one Body Shop product increased considerably when the packaging was changed from a glass jar to a cardboard tube bearing a simple line drawing of a Japanese woman's head and shoulders. The packaging was still minimal and very basic, but the introduction of an effective modern surface graphic on the containers and in promotional cards and window blinds was a major and very effective marketing move. Without turning away from her policy of not wasting resources or money on unnecessary packages, Anita Roddick's expenditure to commission the designs at the forefront of modern trends in graphics has paid for itself.

"Exfoliation – the deliberate removal of dead cells is in our opinion one of the most effective ways of keeping skin looking younger." THE BODY SHOP

Guarantees and Extended Warranties

Motor-vehicle manufacturers recognise that an important aspect of selling a car or truck lies in the guarantees and extended warranties they provide. Volvo in Britain has pioneered new ground by providing 'lifetime care'. Apart from attracting customers, it is also seeking to retain them by offering powerful incentives for their cars to be serviced regularly at approved Volvo dealerships.

Thus, guarantees are a way of attracting and retaining customers, and doubtless you will be aware of examples relating to your business and personal purchases.

| Home-shopping | Tesco set up a scheme for the elderly and disabled in Gateshead, a joint venture between Gateshead Tesco and the University of Newcastle upon Tyne. |
| --- | --- |

Next, which revolutionised High Street shopping in the early 1980s, has done the same for home-shopping with its 'Next Directory'. Next plans to 'break the mould' of the mail-order industry. It has analysed every aspect of the mail-order business to devise a new formula. One aspect is the purchase of Dillons, a chain of newsagents to provide local collection and delivery points.

**Home Videos: Sponsorship**

In America, close to 50 per cent of homes have a video cassette recorder. Many major companies have therefore started to sponsor home videos. Procter & Gamble has sponsored videos based on cable programmes, 'What Every Baby Knows', 'New Born Baby', and 'Advice for New Fathers'. As a sponsorable medium, home video offers a wide range of programme variations to appeal to virtually any group or segment of the market-place. Cascade Swimming Pools has an excellent video on building a DIY pool.

**Joint Promotions**

As its name implies, a joint promotion is one where one or more suppliers benefit from a joint event. A good example is provided by Duracell, which recently won a Marketing Society Award.
*(Industrial Marketing Digest.)*

Duracell set up a number of partnerships with manufacturers in which each helps the other to sell more goods in the shop. This was done on a sector by sector approach, such as toys and security devices.

These and similar promotions advanced the advantages to customers of the in-product battery, and thus the 'added value' of these products.

**Kiosks**

It is common for short-term car rental to be sold from kiosks at railway stations and airports, but there is no reason why similar kiosks could not be erected to sell other products or services, in, for example, shopping malls.

| | |
|---|---|
| Leads Advice | Organising your company to pick up potential leads is clearly part of the customer-attraction process. |
| | If you have a number of people in contact with different departments among your customers, it is important to evolve a system for picking up leads which – if followed up – could result in your gaining business. |
| | Our company has a form on which my colleagues have to submit all their contacts with our clients, so that our administrator can review them, and pick up prospects for future business. |
| | Even in a relatively small company, such a formal system of making sure that you become aware of all potential customers is essential. |
| Leaflet Drops | Local newsagents will often include a leaflet when delivering the morning papers, or voluntary organisations such as the Boy Scouts or commercial organisations can ensure that one of your leaflets or brochures is delivered to every house within a specified area. |
| Logo/Motif | Earlier, I was a little cynical about advertising agencies who are constantly persuading every new client to change their logo. |
| | However, there is no doubt that a strong logo or motif, if properly exploited, can be a way of branding your product or service, whenever it is seen by potential customers. Many companies – as you will have seen – use cartoon style animals as a logo. However, it has to be sufficiently distinctive and consistent to register with prospective customers. |

| Mail Order | Mail order is attempting to attract a new generation of home-shoppers by producing 'specialogues' for clearly defined consumer groups. Some are devised to add younger, more affluent consumers to their traditional markets. |

Freemans portfolio of specialogues — magazine-style catalogues aimed at target groups of customers. They reinforce our fashion strength in agency mail order and spearhead our initiatives in direct mail order.

| Merchandising | Merchandising makes it easy for customers to buy. The Body Shop concept is to group products so that they are easy for the customer to find. When a shop is well merchandised, the eye can easily reach everything, and information labels are clear and easy to read. The skill is to make even the least wanted products say 'come and buy me'. |

Good merchandising should draw your customers into your business by:

- Making your business seem interesting and exciting.

- Offering promotions or incentives.

- Creating a topical interest linked to an event or season of the year.

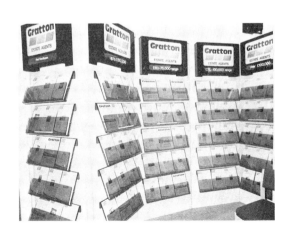

When you go shopping, you can soon decide for yourself which businesses make their merchandising exciting and attractive or positively discouraging. One estate agent has used these principles to good effect.

197

| | |
|---|---|
| Merchandising (Joint) | You can add to the interest of your showroom by joint merchandising displays with other shops and companies. If, for example, you sell Italian cars, you could have a special Italian evening selling Italian leather goods, and a travel agent could market Italian holidays. |
| | In return, if you run a shop to which wives drag their reluctant husbands, you can liaise with the local golf shop to mount a display of greater interest to men. |
| Microvideo | It may be difficult to persuade customers to give up the time needed to visit you, particularly if any degree of travel is required. So it may be necessary to take your factory or operation to your customers. |
| | One company did this very successfully by using a microvideo, which offered portability. A sales representative could sling it over his shoulder, it was battery driven, and above all it is still relatively novel. |
| | It is often possible to interest more than one executive from the customer's organisation in seeing the film and, thus, your company can become known to a broader section of executives likely to influence the decision to buy your product or service. |
| | The cost of the equipment is approximately £1,500 and the average cost of one film works out as being in the area of £7.50 a showing: a modest sum in relation to the average cost of a sales call and the effectiveness of the film. |

| | |
|---|---|
| Mobile Exhibitions | One way of making sure that your customers visit your exhibition stand is to create your own mobile exhibition. |
| | You will have seen for yourself organisations which have kitted up a caravan, a former bus, or even an articulated trailer to use as a touring exhibition. Since it is necessary to phone customers in advance to ask them if they would like to receive the mobile exhibition, it enhances the perception of the visit. It is also an 'event' in the sense that it calls for some preparation by the company to be visited as well as the visitor. If you are visiting a large organisation, you may even need to arrange for posters to be placed in the works canteen or tickets to be issued to the relevant number of executives you wish to see your exhibition. |
| | To be successful, a considerable amount of pre-planning is necessary. |
| | If the company you wish to visit lacks the parking space for your exhibition, you may need to arrange to use the car park of the local hotel. |
| Money-saving Offers | When Honeywell wanted to achieve orders from a mailshot, its mailing was timed to coincide with an annual price increase. The hospitals which responded to the mailshot were allowed a valuable money-saving offer to purchase at the previous price for a further three months, provided they placed their orders before the expiry date of the offer. |
| Newsletters | A firm of architects wanted to get better known. So it started a well produced newsletter giving advice on a range of issues, with illustrations of how it solved similar problems for clients. |
| | A computer software company developed programmes which were particularly relevant to lawyers and accountants. So it started circulating a special newsletter on computers for the legal profession and another for accountants. |
| On-site Displays | If your business requires you to work on different locations, it is important to publicise this in a way which reinforces the perceptions of existing customers, and helps you to gain new customers. |
| | Earlier, we mentioned that Lovell Construction boldly paints its logo on the entrance to all the building and construction sites on which it is working. This made customers aware of the depth and breadth of services which Lovells provided. |

Similarly, you will have seen builders displaying a board outside the house on which they are working, or shopfitters displaying a board when refitting a local shop or bank.

**Opening Hours**

For years, Bowes & Bowes was *the* bookshop in Bath. It opened from 9.00 am to 5.30 pm. Tim Waterstone opened a shop opposite. It stays open to 10 pm five nights a week, enabling bibliophiles to browse at their leisure. Bowes & Bowes has closed. Making it convenient for customers to buy from you at their convenience will always pay.

**Parties**

Tupperware was one of the pioneers of recruiting a lady to organise a party in her home for her friends at which they would be encouraged to buy Tupperware.

Lingerie and leatherware companies have organised similar events.

Men tend to be better served with, for example, membership of their golf club, but getting a group of men with similar business or leisure interests could still be worthwhile.

**Point of Sale**

If you are selling a product or service in a retailing environment, you need to bear in mind that 80 per cent of all sales are achieved from the effectiveness of your 'point of sale' material.

Such items can include clocks, stickers, show cards, leaflets, plus counter and wall display units.

200

| Posters and Hoardings | Posters and hoardings can be on or at a number of different locations: |
|---|---|

**Posters and Hoardings**

Posters and hoardings can be on or at a number of different locations:

- Airports
- Buses and bus shelters
- Driving-school cars
- Parking meters
- Railway stations
- Roadsides
- Sports grounds
- Taxis.

They can be cost-effective.

**Presentations**

If, like me, you are providing a professional service, then you will be very much involved in making presentations to prospective clients.

It is very important to devote a considerable amount of time to pre-planning to ensure that such a presentation enhances the **perception** of your organisation in a way that helps you to build a long-standing relationship.

There are a number of visual aids that can help you do this.

**Brochures** should be designed so that the salesman can use them when making his presentation.

These, the brochure could begin, are our products:

- These are the materials in which they are made.
- These (pointing to pictures which are the closest to the prospect's application) are the different applications/ environments for which we have suitable products.
- Here is how our product works.
- Here are the advantages of our product over its rivals.

If the sales representative uses such a brochure effectively, he will not have to fish around for reasons why the customer should buy; he can anticipate price objections. The effect of such a product brochure would be to restore benefit selling, something that can so easily be lost.

**Presenter.** This at its most basic is a set of boards, the outer two of which can be fixed to form an easel. The remaining boards have professionally produced commentary and illustrations which can be turned over progressively, to aid you in making a logical, illustrated presentation.

**Slide/Cassette.** It is possible to produce a number of slides to illustrate the points you wish to make.

It is also possible to prepare a cassette which can be pulsed at appropriate intervals, so that the slides are changed automatically.

These can be shown on a piece of equipment which is like a miniature mobile television set. This then enables you to have a professional 'voice over' making the case on your behalf, with appropriate illustrations using the slides.

**Microvideos.** As explained earlier, it is possible to have a small microvideo unit some 19 cm across on which to display short microvideo films. These can prove very effective, particularly because, being battery-driven, they can be presented without worrying about leads and points.

**Video.** Of course, more major presentations might justify the use of videos. Many boardrooms have TV and video sets to facilitate such displays, but you will need to check in advance!

Presentations: Third-party Customers

While it is always important to make a good presentation to a potential customer, it becomes even more important when making a presentation to the individuals within a decision-making committee.

Thus, when Four Square Catering was seeking to sell its vending machines to hospitals, it faced a problem. The catering manager might feel that vending tea from a trolley would cost him more money in direct costs, even if it might cost him less in indirect costs.

The domestic manager might be relieved to find that the trollies would take less time but might be sensitive to losing status by not needing so many staff.

Finally, nurses were important because they influence the reaction of patients and might be emotionally committed to the friendliness of the traditional 'cuppa' to the point of resenting the arrival of plastic.

In this instance, Four Square's carefully researched and professionally made video undoubtedly produced far better results than might have been the case had the salesman been left to make individual presentations. *(Industrial Marketing Digest.)*

Presentations: Professional Advisers

The first instinct of many potential customers is to seek the advice of one or more of their professional advisers.

So, when thinking about the way in which you intend to attract these customers, it is worthwhile making a parallel effort aimed at appealing to their professional advisers.

At the same time as the Four Square Catering company was making presentations within hospital units, it was also arranging to make presentations to meetings of such bodies as the Hospital Catering Association and the Institute of Health Service Administrators.

Press Cuttings

Analysing press cuttings can help you to identify and attract business. One construction company, Wilsons, supplements its internally generated information with the systematic screening of fifteen business journals by an assistant in its marketing department. Potentially useful information is then forwarded to the appropriate sales representative. The firm's marketing director once explained that it was interested in what was happening in the market-place of its customers, as much as studying developments in its own market-place.

This total customer orientation extended to maintaining files of press cuttings on its customers. This helped to build relationships based on a better understanding.

**Press Relations**  Pan has an excellent book on the The Body Shop. Chapter nine is devoted to PR. It starts:

> ''The most far-reaching method of projecting a company is, of course, through the media: local and national newspapers, magazines, radio and television. The Body Shop has never spent a penny on advertising space apart from recruitment purposes, yet it has an extremely high media profile and the British public know more background information about The Body Shop than any other toiletries and cosmetic company.
>
> When Anita Roddick opened her first shop, it was in a tiny alleyway shared with two undertakers. A week before she was due to open Anita received a letter from a firm of solicitors complaining that her choice of the name 'The Body Shop' was inappropriate. Initially worried, she then had a brainwave. She made an anonymous telephone call to the local newspaper: 'You'll never guess what is going on in Kensington Gardens . . . a mafia of funeral directors is ganging up on this poor woman who is trying to open a herbal cosmetic shop.' The newspaper printed a centre-spread story. The free publicity of the story ensured a continual stream of interested public into the shop from the first day of trading.
>
> It is estimated that editorial coverage is worth ten times the equivalent space in advertising. The beauty press is courted by the cosmetic companies with expensive gifts and lavish luncheons. This falls under The Body Shop's ban on unnecessary packaging. Despite this, by dedicated hard work, The Body Shop has succeeded.
>
> In the first two years, Anita herself handled all the PR. With characteristic verve she painted The Body Shop logo on her car and raced around speaking to Women's Institute meetings 'every single day, everywhere I could'. She contacted women's magazines such as *Honey* and *Woman's Own* and visited their London offices. She started to have monthly luncheons with members of the beauty press to build an attitude of trust.''

In fact, Chapter nine is a marvellous case study in building a business on PR.


**Press Releases**  We receive dozens of press releases every day. Some have the introverted approach of an organisation so preoccupied with what it is doing that they go straight into the waste paper basket. Others are recognised as being 'extroverted', concerned to present a newsworthy story of interest to our editors and readers. These we start to look out for and to use. But, however good the press releases, it is still necessary to build personal relationships with the journalists writing about your particular trade or industry.

| Promotions | One way of attracting customers is to organise promotions which will draw them to your business. |
|---|---|

A friend, Colin Withers of Bredon Motor Company, organises a regular programme of such promotions. As one example, he held a 'Ladies Evening' in his new car dealership. His own staff prepared the buffet for the nominal cost of the food purchased from the local supermarket. The local ladies' fashion shop gave a fashion parade. A shop selling microwaves gave a demonstration, as did a local hairdresser.

Colin has learnt two lessons on organising these events. First, getting too many people is counter-productive. It is better to get 50 people along and be able to talk to them than to be swamped with 150 people with whom one cannot talk properly.

Secondly, it is a waste of time to rely on posters or even newspaper adverts. The prospective customers you wish to come need to be approached by a specific direct-mail invitation, in a way which encourages them to reply yes or no to your invitation. So, we come back to the need for a complete customer communication system.

| Prospecting | Prospecting is so unpopular with salesmen it may be better to use women, who are more conscientious. |
|---|---|

If it is done properly, it can generate a very warm reaction. One friend located on one of the new science parks actually complained that very few of the local businesses, on whom he depends for supplies, have ever bothered to prospect him.

Prospecting can be done very effectively on the telephone and by a direct-mail campaign which entices the recipient to call to see you to receive a small gift, or to take part in some more worthwhile competition.

If you are building up your customer database, discussed earlier, then prospecting becomes much easier because you can build a regular relationship with everyone who has ever come near your business. Such a system should not neglect your existing customers.

A double glazing manufacturer decided to do a direct-mail campaign to all his existing customers. As a result, more than 12 per cent of them made additional purchases. *(Industrial Marketing Digest.)*

## Public Relations

Public relations helps to build or helps to enhance your position within the particular trade or industry in which you operate.

To talk in local schools about the career prospects of your trade or industry builds a relationship with the children, their teachers, their parents and relatives. Providing a speaker for local organisations such as Rotary and Round Table and others helps build local goodwill.

One important area of public relations, which also helps to motivate your staff, is to support the activities and members of your staff. For example, if they wish to enter the local carnival, lend them a pick-up truck, or your lorry.

Be seen to be making a constructive contribution to the life of the community in which you operate.

## Qualified Leads

How often has your attention been caught by an advertisement suggesting that you write for details? Perhaps it is something you cannot afford, or do not really need, but you write off for details out of idle curiosity.

To send off any worthwhile brochure can cost you a minimum of £3 or £4. To phone up the respondent can cost as much, if not more. To send a salesman can cost anything between £5 and £100, depending on the distance travelled.

So we need to concern ourselves with techniques which produce 'qualified leads'. It may be that we have to take far greater care in designing the reply coupons on our advertisements.

If we use direct mail, we need to take an equal amount of care with the reply cards we include (see below). But, as we will discuss later, perhaps the best way of qualifying leads is by the effective use of the telephone.

For further details regarding availability of stand space please complete and return to:

**SPECTRUM EXHIBITIONS LTD**

Freepost (BR57), Brighton BN2 2ZZ or Tel: (0273) 675131

☐ Please send me details of exhibition space.
☐ Please send me ....... tickets.
☐ Please send me conference details.

NAME:_____

POSITION:_____

COMPANY:_____

ADDRESS:_____ TEL:_____ mim

| Reception Selling | Many trades, industries, and professions require their potential customers to go into a reception area. |
|---|---|

You will know for yourself how daunting this can be. Some areas are dirty, unattractive, with dog-eared magazines and a frosty receptionist who clearly resents your interruption to her duties (or personal activities).

One way of testing your own reception areas is to ask friends to come and visit you by appointment. Then ask them to write a report on how they would have felt had they been a genuine customer visiting you for the purpose of giving you their business.

- How easy was it to follow the signs to the reception area?
- Was the reception area itself attractively and well furnished?
- Were the magazines and newspapers up to date?
- Were they greeted immediately, or were they ignored?
- If they were ignored, was it because the girl was genuinely busy, or because she self-importantly continued with her own affairs?
- Was the eventual greeting warm and friendly and helpful?

Reduced Prices Companies can seek to gain business by special price reductions. But many people do not understand percentages. You may feel that you are being terribly generous to offer a 20 per cent discount, but if your customers cannot understand the benefit, then they are unlikely to be attracted. Prior to Carlzon joining Linjeflyg, it had a youth fare with a 50 per cent discount. This was not particularly successful. On his arrival, Jan Carlzon was told that a further reduction in prices would attract between 3,000 and 5,000 additional customers. But he did not express the new offer as a discounted price. He called it 'Hundred Note', standing for 100 Swedish Krona, and featured the phrase in all his advertising. It pulled in 125,000 additional customers in the first Summer alone. As Jan Carlzon says, 'The story of the Hundred Note affair is proof that running a business is not always a matter of logic and mathematics. It is just as much a question of understanding the psychological impact that a new and intriguing offer will make on the market.'

Referrals Whenever you and I receive exceptionally good service, or feel that we have made a good buy, we are so chuffed about it that we tell our friends and relatives. If we have been forced to complain, and the complaint has been dealt with honourably, then we will tell people about it.

Every one of your customers has relatives, friends, and business associates who could become your customers. What is needed is to evolve a campaign which will motivate them to take positive action to introduce their contacts to you.

Austin Rover wrote a direct-mail letter to prospective purchasers of their new model. They offered a £250 voucher to the recipient and a further £250 for them to give to a friend. If their customer database showed that the prospects had recently purchased a car, then they sent two vouchers, each of £250 for them to give to two of their friends.

| Replacement Back-up | If the continued operation of the product you sell is vital to your customer, then it may be necessary to offer a replacement product in the event of a breakdown. |
|---|---|

As more companies become increasingly reliant on their computers for the smooth running of their businesses, then the breakdown of their computer becomes a disaster; so those providing computer hardware and software need to be able to provide back-up facilities.

| Reply Cards | Many industrial markets are fragmented, making it difficult to home in on precise potential areas for sales. Moreover, if your product is new or you have developed wider applications for an existing product, where can you find the information you need about the potential customers, and their reactions to your product? |
|---|---|

The answer is to do a direct-mail campaign to suitable prospects and to make full use of that valuable item . . . the reply card! Make your reply card work for you by asking for the information that will give you qualified leads.

**3M Griddle Cleaning System.** This is a low cost, purpose-made product which 3M wanted to publicise in a way which would produce a high level of qualified leads for their distributors. This was particularly important because, with the enormous number of products sold by distributors, it is difficult for everyone to be given sufficient attention. It was decided to test-mail a list with a high proportion of fast food outlets, but which also included traditional catering establishments such as pubs, restaurants, canteens, and cafeterias.

To obtain a **free sample** of the griddle cleaning system, recipients were asked to complete a simple reply card. Respondents were asked to indicate, from a tick-box selection, the type of outlet, number of griddles used, current methods of cleaning, and the name of their cleaning material supplier.

Without exception all cards returned were completed in full, and the analysis of the response gave 3M a great deal of valuable information, including:

- the incidence of griddles in establishments other than fast food outlets, widening the potential market.

- the majority of griddles were being cleaned in a way which would damage their surface, indicating a major selling point.

- suppliers named were already 3M distributors, making lead conversion easier.

The response rate was over 10 per cent, accomplished on a low budget, which would not have supported a trade advertising campaign. *(Industrial Marketing Digest.)*

Reputation

It can take a long time to establish, but it can be destroyed quickly by the wrong executives or employees; thus an extremely important asset of your business is your reputation.

You need to plan carefully the ways in which you will build your reputation, you need to be able to monitor the activities which affect it closely, and, should something occur to damage it, you need to respond quickly.

Roadshows:
Displays

If you are selling through distributors or dealers, it is often essential to support their efforts to attract the customers to buy your products. One way of doing this is to have a travelling 'Roadshow'. The Unipart organisation ran a very successful series of Roadshows. This included a stage presentation by professional dancers and comedians to provide real entertainment value for the visitors. In addition, the visitors were entitled to tour a mini-exhibition which included the design and layout of the shops, fitting, and merchandise which Unipart was recommending to its potential franchisees.

This was a major exercise in logistics, with a number of lorries needed to transport the demonstration equipment, ready-mounted displays, films, videos, and other presentation items, which were set up in turn, in a number of appropriate hotel and conference facilities throughout Britain.

*A full 2-hour 'West End'-style production gave Unipart employees all the facts on the company's privatisation plans.*

**Sales: Administration**

The ease, or the difficulty, with which you handle the administration of the sale is important to your customers. I once rebelled. The local store was offering nine months interest-free credit. We bought a carpet, then I was told that I would be expected to walk some distance through the store, up a back stairway, into a grotty office to complete the forms. I would then have been required to walk back to the carpet department to show them the signed documentation.

I refused and demanded that if they were doing a promotion based on free credit, they should train the staff concerned to complete the formalities!

**Sales: Follow-up**

Have you ever replied to an advertising or direct-mail campaign, perhaps for a product which has excited you, or has seemed the answer to one of your problems? How quickly were you contacted? Was it quickly enough to build on your initial interest, or so delayed that you had either lost interest, or solved your problem by buying another product? Have there been occasions when you did not even receive a reply?

The problem with some advertising or direct-mail campaigns is that they are **too successful**. The company concerned is so overwhelmed with replies that it cannot cope, it farms out the replies to local salesmen without any discipline to ensure that the proper follow-up procedures are applied.

It is not only a waste of money, but can adversely affect your relationship with prospective customers, if you do not follow up promptly.

It may be a process of trial and error but it is worthwhile limiting the number of direct-mail letters or adverts you place until you gain a picture of the number of replies and thus can programme your team so that it is able to follow up the leads promptly.

Sales: Training

Your success in business will depend on the quality of the executives and employees with whom your customers come into contact.

Training in customer relations is a constant, 'drip-feed' approach which permeates the whole organisation. Attitudes cannot be changed overnight. Many technically or professionally qualified people still regard selling as 'dirty'. The opposite is the case. '**Good selling is good serving**.'

You and all those who work with you should be absolutely enthusiastic about selling the benefits of your product or service to your customers.

Secondary Packaging

All too often, the care spent on nicely presented boxes of your product can be spoilt if the retailer had to split the box to supply units individually. One company called Tuckers sells fixing bolts called Parabolts which are normally purchased by small builders. So Tuckers' distributors were supplied with rolls (and dispensers) of red, white, and blue plastic bags. These bore not only the slogan and logo of Tuckers, but also an application message: 'Fast, Secure Fixings in Concrete, Brick, Blocks and Stone.' *(Industrial Marketing Digest.)*

Since the bags get used for everything, a constant stream of low-cost Parabolt bags flows out through the distributors' stores.

Seminars

Kwik-Fit hosts a series of seminars organised by the Institute of Trading Standards. These seminars provide a forum for representatives of both organisations to exchange information on their common objectives of consumer protection and satisfaction, and are designed to promote greater understanding and co-operation and higher standards within the industry.

Service Engineers

Everyone in your company depends on the sales you achieve from your customers, including your service engineers. They, too, need to be trained in the techniques of customer relations. Indeed, it can be a good idea to make sure that your service engineers are trained in the same way and at the same time as your salesmen.

Your service engineer can give you invaluable information on what is going on within the business of your customers. He meets and influences people who may be even unknown to your salesman. He can carry out **research** on the acceptability or otherwise of your products or services. He can carry out in-house customer training to ensure that they derive maximum benefit from your product or service. He can help with your customer relations generally. He will often be the first one to know that your customer is expanding, and may therefore need additional equipment.

One of the problems is you may be paying your salesmen attractive rates of commission and such substantially enhanced benefits as a good car, whereas your service engineers may be regarded as 'blue collar' workers on a flat salary who drive around in a van.

To get the best from your service engineers, you have to make them feel part of the team by giving them public recognition and appreciation. You may need to consider some formal bonus scheme on leads converted, or have some competition prizes for their contribution to attracting, satisfying, and retaining your customers.

The same points apply to any other employees who come into contact with customers, be they parts department staff, accounts department staff, secretaries, telephonists, or delivery van drivers.

Showcases
While these are normally found in shops, if you have an interesting product or service you may be able to get local shops, railway stations, hotels or similar organisations to let you put your showcase on display either temporarily or permanently.

Signs: Fascia
Walk down the High Street of your town and mark out of ten all the shopfront signs you see. Carry out the same exercise in your local trading estate. If necessary, take photographs. What impressions do these signs give you and your colleagues? Some amateurishly painted signs give the impression of a low cost, unprofessional business. Signs with letters missing indicate that management is not taking care of detail. Now do an evaluation of your own signs. Take some photographs and ask some of your customers what impression they derive from the way in which you have presented your business.

| | |
|---|---|
| Signs: Internal | Would a visitor to your business get an immediate impression of where to park his car, and where to go to find the right department or executive? I am sure that you often get a bit irritated and confused when you seek to find your way to the office or department you need. |
| Signs: Directions | How easy do you make it for your customers to find their way to do business with you? Sometimes, town planning regulations may inhibit, but it may well be worthwhile using posters to make sure that customers know how to find you.  |

Specialogues

This is a new approach to mail-order which Step Four adopted by focusing on specific groups. Thus, Littlewoods has French Connection, Moods, Top Man and Q & A, in addition to Changes.

Freemans initiated the trend of large A3 catalogues of less than 50 pages which offer a neater and more co-ordinated range of items than appear in traditional catalogues.

Sponsorship

This is not a direct way of attracting customers to you, but of creating an awareness of your business. Often the degree of awareness gained depends on the extent of the media coverage you gain.

One sponsorship which gained favourable reviews was when Digital, one of the world's largest computer companies, decided to revive the Schneider Trophy Air Race. *(Industrial Marketing Digest.)*

What Digital decided it wanted was greater visibility for its name. This meant media exposure. Digital chose a scheme that lent itself to multiple and repeated exposure which its PR consultancy, Infopress, diligently and imaginatively applied itself to obtain.

Stock Levels

If you are in a business selling any item from stock, the depth, breadth, and availability of items from stock is a key element in attracting and retaining customers.

| | |
|---|---|
| Telemarketing | The Burton Group subsidiary, Nationwide Credit Company, is using telemarketing to prospect for business among Burtons' 3 million credit-card holders. The new division will be based on the multi-quote system, using an IBM computer. People who are telephoned can be given a quote immediately for any financial product and can be given immediate cover if they have a credit card from Burtons or a major bank. Burtons will also have all details of its customers easily accessible on its computer screens. |
| Telephone | The telephone is one of the most underrated of aids for identifying, attracting, satisfying, and retaining customers. |
| | Yet how many companies set out to train every executive and employee who is required to receive phone calls from, or make phone calls to, customers? |
| Telereception | The first point of contact for customers of your company is often the girl on your switchboard. |
| | We are lucky, we have a marvellously cheerful and effective girl, and it is a pleasure to pass on to her the compliments I receive from my clients. |
| | But how often do you ring up your suppliers as a customer and feel happy with the way in which your phone call is answered? |
| | Indeed, how many times do you ring your own company to 'mystery shop' the way in which your own customers are handled? |
| Telequalifying | As mentioned earlier, it is important to find some way of qualifying the leads you gain so that you can decide how best to approach genuine customers. This is a very effective use of the telephone. |
| | My wife was once given 25 moribund sales leads of customers who had called in on one of our clients some months earlier but had failed to confirm a purchase. She was able to reactivate a dialogue with five of these customers, which resulted in one immediate sale. |
| | A company specialising in this field called – appropriately – Lead Qualification Services once secured an order worth £280,000 for an engineering computer software house from a moribund sales lead which it reactivated. *(Industrial Marketing Digest.)* |
| | Another company specialising in this field, Teleprons, was asked to contact local authorities to: |

- Identify the decision-maker with the authority responsible for purchasing pneumatic drills.

- Find out where he was based.

- Find out what kind of equipment the authority was currently using.

- Ascertain the purchase budget for the coming year, and the year after.

- Make appointments with the hottest prospects while sending literature to others.

The benefit of this Telepron campaign was that appointments were fixed for the salesmen to call on sixty-seven authorities, of whom forty-five made purchases.

What has stimulated the growth in telequalifying services of this type is the expense of a sales force. It can be far more cost-effective to hire disciplined outside specialists to update customer records, generate sales leads, or qualify sales leads and to make appointments on behalf of your sales team.

Teleresearch

Our friends at Herring Son and Daw – a long-established London firm of Chartered Surveyors – wanted to compile a sort of 'Domesday Book' of all major office blocks along the M25 motorway. Three post-graduates photographed each significant building and tape recorded the names of the owners and tenants. Teleresearch then established the terms of the tenancy agreements plus details of the leaseholders and freeholders.

While this exercise was primarily concerned with identifying potential customers, when these prospective customers were approached, they were impressed to find out how much Herring Son and Daw knew about their particular circumstances and thus it was easier to convert them into actual customers.

Telesales

The telephone can be used on a cost-effective basis to attract customers. For more than 10 years my own organisation has had a telesales team both to gain clients and to build relationships with them.

When Herring Son and Daw opened a new Reading office, it used a telemarketing company called Salespoint to make itself known. First, its own staff compiled a list of occupiers of office blocks and factories worth contacting. Telephone numbers were established, and the organisation was rung to find out the name of the executive responsible for managing the property. Then the telemarketing

216

organisation – Salespoint – rang them to explain the history, the skills, and the benefits of using Herring Son and Daw. Over 60 effective contacts were made and nine appointments secured for one of the partners to visit the organisation concerned. Fees from just one of these appointments exceeded £20,000, against a charge from Salespoint of less than £400!

Uniforms

Anita Roddick of The Body Shop has learned five things from the SAS (Special Air Services) in terms of her approach to retailing. One is that the SAS create an aura around their uniform by never allowing it to be worn off duty. There is tremendous pride in wearing the uniform and this is reinforced by such rules.

In many shops and other businesses it is extremely difficult to recognise the staff and this can create customer uncertainty and dissatisfaction.

Unloading Services

If you are providing a somewhat bulky product to your customers, then a convenient unloading service may then be an attraction.

Many organisations in this situation now have hydraulic winches to help with unloading. Many companies now use a special fork-lift truck which is carried on the delivery lorry and is then unloaded first so that it can help to ensure that the products being delivered are placed precisely where the customer wants them.

**Vehicle Liveries**

If your organisation uses vehicles, it is important to use them as travelling advertisements. Study the vans and lorries you see as you travel the roads and motorways in your area. How many truly 'sell' the product or service of their companies? Some you will find to be dirty and some will be very smart and attractively painted, but will not give you any information about the company or its products, or how to buy them. You will see the occasional vehicle which does sell the benefits of the products or services of the company concerned, and give a freefone number to make it easier for the prospective customer to find out more information.

**Video**

At a quoted cost of £1,000 or more per minute, the cost of producing a video may be deemed prohibitively expensive.

However, the cost has to be divided into a cost per customer, or even a cost per sale achieved.

The Lovell construction company used a professionally produced video almost as a mass market 'mail shot' with excellent results. The cost per video sent to each customer was less than £15 but it has to be remembered that Lovell can be quoting for major construction jobs, so gaining one contract would more than cover the cost of the mail shot.

| Videodem | Combining TV and computer technology, this enables customers to ask the questions they may have about your products and services. |

| Visits (Business) | Recently, as an exercise in goodwill and informing the public, British Nuclear Fuels has been advertising on TV that it welcomes visitors to its nuclear power stations. |

An enterprising farmer in a country area concluded that the 'townies' visiting the neighbourhood did not really understand farming life. He therefore promoted farm visits and had a steady stream of paying visitors agog at the livestock and machinery of his farm. Similarly, many people are interested in how things are made and would welcome a chance to be shown around.

Even if you could not handle individual visitors, you might well be able to invite the local Rotarian, Ladies Inner Wheel, and similar organisations. You could liaise with local schools to show parties of schoolchildren around your business.

| Welcoming Newcomers | If you rely primarily on personal or business customers from your area, it is important that you should be aware of newcomers. Estate agents may be willing to help with details of the houses being purchased. The Chamber of Commerce will often publish a list of new members. In one way or another you will need to make sure that you make the first contact with the new arrivals to your market territory. |

| | |
|---|---|
| Window Display (3rd Party) | If you are not a retailer but have an interesting product or service, you can often persuade a local store or building society to let you mount a display for a period. |
| Window Blinds | One of the innovations introduced by The Body Shop is window blinds with a design promoting the product. With dashing modern graphics, the backdrop catches the eye and draws it to a window full of the particular product it displays. |
| Window Display (Your Own) | Anita Roddick of The Body Shop intends to concentrate on window design as a major way of attracting customers into her shops. The window should become a topic of discussion; people should stop and say 'that's interesting'. |
| | Windows are an important factor in designing the image of a town. They create an image of a street, and those of The Body Shop are sought after by shop developers for their attractive and contemporary look. You will never find a Body Shop next to a discount store: it is more likely by a design-conscious shop such as Next. |
| | Early in my career I did the windows for a traditional chemist. He wanted one bottle of everything he sold in the window. This took time and had no impact, since the display was not changed very often. I persuaded him to let me fill it with just one product and change the display twice a week. People stopped to look, more people came in, and sales went up! |

# INTEGRATING YOUR APPROACH

| | |
|---|---|
| | One of the problems of running a company is that as you appoint different managers to run different activities, they became jealous of each other. The danger is that they will often spend more time fighting each other than serving the customers. |
| Confusing Customers | If they have separate departmental budgets, they will often set out to attract customers in different ways. They may position their department and create perceptions which conflict with those you are striving to achieve for your company. |

| Integrated Approach | Clearly, you need to organise your selling activities so that they reinforce each other. |
|---|---|

- Some customers will only buy an item of equipment if they can be confident of good after-sales service.

- Conversely, customers who have been pleased with your service facilities are more likely to buy their next item of equipment from you.

- Understandably, most customers will only buy a major item of equipment if they are satisfied that they can keep it running because you provide a high level of parts availability, and a fast service.

- Conversely, a reputation for good replacement parts service will sell your original equipment.

All the activities of your company should be inter-related and mutually complementary and supportive, so that each product or service reinforces the other products and services.

| Organisation | This has implications on the way in which you organise your business, as we discussed earlier. |
|---|---|

# THE COST OF ATTRACTING CUSTOMERS

| Learning by Experience | As we have now seen, attracting customers is a complex, time-consuming, and highly skilled task. It can only be managed effectively with accurate information which enables you to select the best and most cost-effective method of attracting customers. We all need to learn by experience. |
|---|---|

| Measuring Cost-effectiveness | It is vital that you are able to measure the cost-effectiveness of each method of attracting customers: |
|---|---|

- How much has each individual activity cost?

- How many responses were achieved?

- If the level of responses achieved was low, what lessons can be learned: was it the method itself, or the effectiveness with which it was applied?

- How many of these responses were contacted?

221

- What were the cost and the effectiveness of converting responses into prospects, and if the conversion factor was too low, was it because it took too long to contact respondents, or because the conversion into a prospect was mishandled?

- From these prospects, how many orders were secured?

- What was the cost of the order secured, and if the volume and value was too low, was this the fault of the sales staff or some other fault with the product being offered? For this purpose, you need to regard your product as 'everything the purchaser gets in exchange for his money'.

**Involvement of Accountants**

One of the problems behind some of the preceding questions is that the sales and/or marketing manager needs information from your computer system, or from your financial department, but all too often your accounts department may be unable or unwilling to provide the customer-related information you need.

**A 'F.I.T.' Accountant**

The problem with much of British industry is that accountants tend to be the ones primarily responsible for providing management information when their whole approach to life is geared to financially orientated information. In my view, you cannot afford an accountant who takes such a narrow view of his responsibilities. Our own financial director is in charge of Finance, Information, and Technology. He is in charge of our computers and uses them to provide us with customer-related information.

**Your Top Executive**

I hope the preceding pages will have reinforced the fact that **attracting your customers** is an extremely important and highly skilled business which needs to be given the utmost priority and be the responsibility of one of your top executives.

# 9

# SATISFY YOUR CUSTOMERS

That you **SATISFY** your customers by monitoring closely their reactions to the way in which you seek to meet their needs and wants through your own 'Customer Satisfaction Index'.

## A MOMENT OF TRUTH

Important Flight

'Rudy Peterson was an American businessman staying at the Grand Hotel in Stockholm. One day he left the hotel to accompany a colleague on a Scandinavian Airline flight to Copenhagen. The trip was only for the day, but it was important.

Forgotten Ticket

'When he arrived at the airport, he realised he'd left his ticket back at the hotel. Everyone knows you can't board an aeroplane without a ticket, so he had already resigned himself to missing the flight and his business meeting in Copenhagen. But when he explained his dilemma to the ticket agent, he got a pleasant surprise.

'Don't Worry'

' "Don't worry, Mr Peterson," she said with a smile. "Here's your boarding card. I'll insert a temporary ticket in here. If you just tell me your room number at the Grand Hotel and your destination in Copenhagen, I'll take care of the rest."

Ticket Collected

'While Rudy and his colleague waited in the passenger lounge, the ticket agent dialled the hotel, the bellhop checked his room and found the ticket. The ticket agent then sent an SAS car to retrieve it from the hotel and bring it directly to her. They moved so quickly that the ticket arrived before the Copenhagen flight departed. No one was more surprised than Rudy Peterson when the flight attendant approached him and said calmly, "Mr Peterson? Here's your ticket."

No Ticket, No Flight

'What would have happened at a more traditional airline? Most airline manuals are clear: "No ticket, no flight." Rudy Peterson almost certainly would have missed his flight. Instead, because of the way SAS handled his situation, he was both impressed and on time for his meeting.'

Proud | Jan Carlzon, President of Scandinavian Airlines, starts his marvellous book *Moment of Truth* with this story. He concludes:

'I'm very proud of the Rudy Peterson story because it reflects what we have been able to achieve at SAS in the six years since I became president. We have re-orientated ourselves to become a customer-driven company – a company that recognises that its only true assets are satisfied customers, all of whom expect to be treated as individuals and who won't select us as their airline unless we do just that.'

15-second Contacts | Jan Carlzon adds, 'Last year, each of our ten million customers came in contact with approximately five SAS employees, and this contact lasted an average of 15 seconds each time. Thus, SAS is ''created'' in the minds of our customers, 50 million times a year, 15 seconds a time.'

This reinforces the need to give more responsibility to customer-facing employees.

## THE UNFORTUNATE CONTRAST

Red Star | A colleague took a parcel down to the local Red Star office, some 40 minutes before the next train was due to depart. Three porters were in the office. One said he could not help because he was a trainee. The second said he could not help because he was on official rest-break. The third said he could not help because if he were to take the parcel up to the platform, the office would be left unattended!

Clearly, Sir Robert Reid and his colleagues at British Rail have a mammoth problem of changing attitudes.

## BOSSES COME LAST

Leaders are Watched | Again Jan Carlzon has some very pertinent comments:

'A leader's ways are watched carefully and adopted by others in the organisation. Through their behaviour in turn the leader's personality starts to permeate the entire company.'

He explains that when travelling, his staff would try to give him the best seat. He would refuse this and be happy to accept any seat left after customers were seated.

'If you indicate by your actions that you are superior even to your customers, then you hardly call yourself market oriented.

'At SAS we pass out magazines and newspapers on the aircraft. We do not always have enough for everyone. Sometimes staff try to be kind by offering me my pick first. ''Out of the question,'' I tell them, ''I cannot take any myself until I know that all the passengers have got what they want.''

'By demonstrating that we ourselves come last after the customers, we are telling our employees and the customers what the ranking order really is.'

# MEASURING RESULTS

Customers' View of Performance
The SAS cargo division has always measured its performance by the amount of cargo it carried, but this had nothing to do with the needs of its customers.

As with Richard Gabriel, customers are concerned about efficiency: prompt deliveries to specified locations.

SAS decided to test its own efficiency. It sent 100 packages to various addresses throughout Europe. The results were devastating. The parcels were due to arrive the next day. In fact, the average was 4 days.

Again Jan Carlzon deals with the problem openly and – more importantly – discusses how SAS introduced customer-related measurements.

Measuring Promises
'We had caught ourselves in one of the most basic mistakes service-oriented businesses can make; promising one thing and measuring another. In this case we were promising prompt and precise cargo delivery, yet we were measuring volume and whether or not paperwork and packages got separated.

'Clearly, we needed to start measuring our success in terms of promises.

'QualiCargo'
'So we asked our cargo people to come up with a new method of measuring. They devised the QualiCargo system which measures the precision of our service: how quickly do we answer the telephone? Did we meet the proper deadline? Did the cargo go with the plane we booked it on? How long did it take from the time the plane landed until the cargo was ready to be collected by the customer?

225

| Inter Unit Comparisons | 'The results of the measurements are published every month. A QualiCargo diagram included in each report compares the various cargo terminals with each other and with their own targets. It graphically shows which station has done the best and which has done the worst. Today we are up to 92 per cent precision. |

| People's New Understanding | 'Are our staff working harder than before? No. The SAS cargo staff has always worked with intensity and dedication. Now that a more accurate system of measurement has identified previously unrecognised problems, routines have been changed and resources have been shifted. |

'The major improvement in precision and speed . . . arose from the cargo people's new understanding of what is important to SAS customers.'

## ENSURING PEOPLE UNDERSTAND

| Objective | The last point made by Jan Carlzon is important. He accepts that his people always worked with 'intensity and dedication'. |

The problem was that top management had let them down by not providing them with a clear understanding of their objectives, nor of the measurements they needed to check their own performance.

| Over-conscientious! | The majority of people go to work with the intention of doing their best. Where they mishandle customers, it is often with the best of intentions. |

Jim Maxmin of Thorn-EMI discussed the point at one of our client meetings. If customer-facing staff have been trained to think purely in terms of profit, then they will be reluctant to give way to a customer, even on 20p. As a result, the business loses the customer's lifetime goodwill. Jim went on:

'You must allow your staff to make a trade-off between profit and customer satisfaction. This is critical.

'We have in our rental business, some 4 million customers. In one year we estimated that we lost 25,000 customers in disputes over money. So I had this quantified. The total cost, if we had given in to every complaint, would have been £36,000 on a turnover of

£982 million! Some poor sod out there thought he was doing what I wanted to make money. So it's my fault that we lost those customers. The average customer produces for us about £225 a year in revenue. So, you've got to make the choice of priorities – customers or profit – and give your staff their guidelines on your philosophy.'

# CREATING THE RIGHT ORGANISATION

Front-line
Responsibility

Customer satisfaction depends, ultimately, on the quality of the product or service the customer has purchased. But the most marvellous product or service in the world will be spoilt if the customer is handled badly. Conversely, the more average product or service can be enhanced if the customer is handled in a way which gives him, or her, a great deal of satisfaction and pleasure.

So, the only way to gain a competitive advantage is to give far greater responsibility to those of our employees and executives who are in 'front-line' contact with customers.

Customer
Liaison Teams

As we discussed in Step Seven, you may need to create totally new systems of organisation to ensure total customer satisfaction.

Sir Colin Marshall of British Airways initiated an attitude-changing training programme for all his executives and employees.

He has also initiated unique 'Customer Liaison Teams'. These teams patrol the arrival and departure lounges. Anyone looking lost or bewildered is approached as a part of BA's policy of caring for customers on the ground as well as in the air. BA is the first airline to operate such a scheme and team members say they will help passengers travelling with other airlines.

Are there ways in which you could improve liaison between your customers and your company?

Measurement
Essential

But, if front-line employees are to be given more responsibility, they must also be given the measurements by which their results will be judged.

# CUSTOMER-SATISFACTION INDEX

Measurement
Essential

If the key aspect of our business is the satisfaction of customers, we ought to have some objective way of measuring whether or not we are succeeding.

We need a 'customer-satisfaction index'.

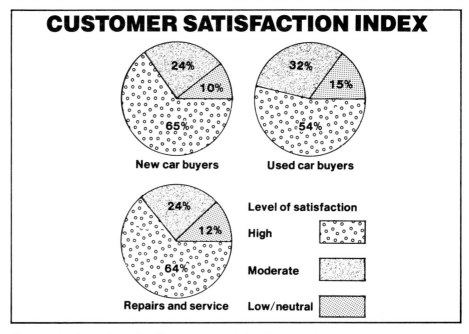

**CUSTOMER SATISFACTION INDEX**

New car buyers: 24%, 10%, 65%

Used car buyers: 32%, 15%, 54%

Repairs and service: 24%, 12%, 64%

Level of satisfaction

High

Moderate

Low/neutral

Encouraging Complaints

One technique is to be far more positive in creating a climate in which customers are encouraged to complain.

Tom Farmer gives 'satisfaction cards' to every customer and some 40 per cent of customers complete them. These are analysed daily at Tom's headquarters in Edinburgh. In 1986 his level of complaints was equivalent to .001 per cent, or one complaint per 10,000 customers. Not bad going!

Satisfaction Cards

You, like me, will have seen the cards which hotels often display in bedrooms. These cards ask us to comment on the standard of service received. I do not know what percentage of guests bother, but they are now so much 'part of the furniture' that I doubt that the percentage is very high.

Definite Programme

What is needed is a programme to make sure that all our customers, those who are pleased as well as those who are displeased, take the time and trouble to complete an objective questionnaire on the extent to which we have satisfied them. This will not be achieved by the general issue of a satisfaction card. It needs to be a specific action where we give a card or write a direct-mail letter enclosing a questionnaire. Some companies offer some small incentive or prize to customers who complete the questionnaire.

If you can achieve a **customer-satisfaction index** of between 80 per cent and 85 per cent, you are probably doing extremely well.

# CUSTOMER SATISFACTION STARTS WITH THE 'BOSS'

Kwik-Fit

One boss who accepts that customer satisfaction starts through his personal example is Tom Farmer, who has built his Kwik-Fit organisation into a company which in 1986 achieved sales of over £100 million and a return on total capital employed of over 34 per cent.

Tom very kindly spoke at one of our client meetings and I am grateful for permission to quote from the highlights of his talk.

---

## KEEPING CLOSE TO CUSTOMERS: TOM FARMER

Kwik-Fit Posters

The poster shown opposite is displayed in all Kwik-Fit service areas, offices and warehouses and its contents constantly remind every member of our staff who it is who pays our wages and the importance of 'keeping close to the customer'.

In every business, the most important person associated with that business is the customer, for if there are no customers, there is no business and no need for staff, suppliers, premises or marketing, or financial policies and procedures.

100 Per Cent Customer Satisfaction

Keeping close to the customer is giving what he or she wants which is '100 per cent customer satisfaction' at all times.

**OUR CODE OF PRACTICE MEANS THAT THE STAFF OF THIS DEPOT WILL:-**

- ☑ Treat your vehicle with care and fit protective seat covers.
- ☑ Examine your vehicle with you and give an honest appraisal of work required.
- ☑ Give, on request, a binding quotation before work commences.
- ☑ Ensure that all work is carried out in accordance with the Company's laid down procedures.
- ☑ Inform you immediately of any complications or delays.
- ☑ Examine all finished work with you before your vehicle leaves the premises.
- ☑ Make available to you, on request, all parts removed from your vehicle.

---

**1986: THE YEAR OF THE CUSTOMER.**

# I am your customer

I am your customer. Satisfy my wants – add personal attention and a friendly touch – and I will become a walking advertisement for your products and services. Ignore my wants, show carelessness, inattention and poor manners, and I will simply cease to exist – as far as you are concerned.

I am sophisticated. Much more so than I was a few years ago. My needs are more complex. I have grown accustomed to better things. I have money to spend. I am an egotist. I am sensitive; I am proud. My ego needs the nourishment of a friendly, personal greeting from you. It is important to me that you appreciate my business. After all, when I buy your products and services, my money is feeding you.

I am a perfectionist. I want the best I can get for the money I spend. When I criticise your products or service – and I will, to anyone who will listen, when I am dissatisfied – then take heed. The source of my discontent lies in something you or the products you sell have failed to do. Find that source and eliminate it or you will lose my business and that of my friends as well.

I am fickle. Other businessmen continually beckon to me with offers of "more" for my money. To keep my business, you must offer something better than they. I am your customer now, but you must prove to me again and again that I have made a wise choice in selecting you, your products and services above all others.

**Our aim is 100% Customer Satisfaction**

| | |
|---|---|
| **Successful Service Companies** | Successful service companies are those who stay close to the customer. |
| | They have fully trained staff not just trained in the technical aspects of the job but trained in the art of communications: how to communicate with a customer. Many problems between motorists and service outlets are due to bad communication and I believe that the most important ingredient for success in the service industry is training. |
| **81 Per Cent Customer Loss** | In a survey carried out in America, it was shown that out of every 100 customers a retail/service business has today, it will lose 81 per cent within the next 10 years – 67 per cent will be lost because of discourteous and indifferent treatment, another 14 per cent are lost because faults are not settled correctly. This means 81 per cent of those people lost are lost because of bad communication. |
| | Astonishing figures when we consider the millions of pounds spent on advertising, premises and equipment etc., all money spent to bring customers to our doors to service or not to service. |
| | They are the customers who pay our wages and are lost because they are taken for granted – lost because of not having and carrying out a philosophy of customer care and 100 per cent satisfaction. |
| **Identify, Anticipate, Satisfy** | But '100 per cent customer satisfaction' is easier to say than to achieve, because we now are in the field of human behaviour – behaviour of people who are served and the people who serve them. We must first of all identify what are the needs of those being served, then we must identify, anticipate, and satisfy these customer requirements profitably. |
| **Right Service** | But I would add to that one more dimension and that is coupled with right service. |
| **Customer Orientation** | But for management to talk of good servicing and 'staying close to the customer' is not good enough; we must ensure that every member in the company is customer-orientated. Service must devolve upon every member of staff from the telephonist, who is the first point of contact, through the mechanic, salesman, commercial director, customer liaison department or whoever it may be that's on the receiving end of an enquiry or a complaint – the list is endless because it's everybody on the payroll. |

| | |
|---|---|
| Company Philosophy | Once we appreciate this fundamental fact, we realise that to talk of service means also to talk of personnel policies, of internal communications, of motivation and involvement – in fact to lay bare the philosophy of the company and how the company deals with staff relations, that is with the human being whose job and future depends on the company's success. |
| | Now it seems obvious to me that you cannot expect your staff to behave differently to the manner in which the company behaves to them. Customers and staff are the head and tail of the same coin. And the way you treat the whole of that coin depends on your philosophy of business. |
| | The achievement of 100 per cent customer satisfaction embraces all aspects of the retailers' role I referred to earlier and it is the way the customer is dealt with by staff he remembers, talks about and either recommends or does not. |
| Management Commitment | To get that message down the line to staff needs commitment from top management to training and good communications. It's not difficult to discover what your customer thinks of you and your service. |
| | Directors and all senior personnel have only to visit their workshops and offices and talk to their staff and their customers with seeing eyes and listening ears – and that means looking objectively, not seeing what one wants to see or translating what people are saying into what one wants to hear. |
| Customer Research | Research into customers' attitudes to the company must be carried out by the careful monitoring of customer satisfaction cards given out to every customer who has work done. The standard of service must be monitored thoroughly and immediate action taken when necessary. |
| | Regular market research must be carried out to keep management fully informed of trends and effectiveness of advertising and other information necessary to ensure success. |
| Complaints | Unfortunately, there are times when something goes wrong and a customer has justification in making a complaint. These complaints must be dealt with speedily and efficiently, and if handled properly, those customers who are dealt with to their complete satisfaction will be able to claim they did achieve 100 per cent customer satisfaction. |

It is interesting to note that Gallup Poll recently found out that in the holiday business a dissatisfied customer will tell eleven people of his problems but a satisfied customer will only tell four people the good news.

This means that, just to stand still, holiday companies must have three times more satisfied than dissatisfied customers. I wonder what these figures would be in the motor trade.

Year of the Customer

To reinforce our commitment to providing the highest standards of service, 1986 was designated 'The Year of the Customer'. Every member of staff was constantly reminded of the need to achieve our aim '100 per cent customer satisfaction' at all times.

Success Formula

In conclusion, 'staying close to the customer' must be the guiding principle of any business. The successful ones will acknowledge that customers are the be all and end all of a business.

Customers' loyalty will be achieved by ensuring:

- Good locations
- Well trained staff
- Value for money
- Dedication to achieving 100 per cent customer satisfaction.

Our own company operates these principles and I know that these principles have been the reason for its success.

Success or failure is essentially a matter of human relationships.

It is the reaction to us from our family – customers, employers and employees and associates.

If the reaction is favourable, we are likely to succeed – if it is unfavourable, we are doomed.

## 10 RETAIN AND UPGRADE YOUR CUSTOMERS

That you **RETAIN** your customers by conscious retention policies the success of which is measured by your 'Customer Retention Index', and that you continuously **UPGRADE** the way in which you meet customer needs and wants by keeping ahead of their expectations in a rapidly changing environment; and thus achieve your **VISION.**

## POST-PURCHASE DISSATISFACTION

'Cognitive Dissonance'
This is another 'buzz' expression, but it is important for all that. It is human nature that, having made a major purchase, most of us go through a period of post-purchase uncertainty.

If our friends and colleagues praise our choice, we feel boosted and confirmed in our wisdom. But if a valued contact starts to express doubts or reservations, our own reservations flood in.

'Post-purchase Follow-up'
Thus the post-purchase 'follow-up' is important when you make a major sale. The sales department should ensure that the purchaser is visited or phoned within four or five days of his purchase, to make sure that everything is satisfactory. Apart from the goodwill value of such a follow-up, it can also be an opportunity to get four or five referrals and introductions to friends and relatives.

Similarly, if your customers have their purchase serviced, it can be a worthwhile investment to ring up a day or two later to make sure that they are happy with the service and no problems have arisen.

## RETAINING CUSTOMERS

One cynic alleges that while most businesses are quite good at gaining customers, they are even better at losing them! Therefore an important '**key performance standard**' for your business is your '**customer retention rate**':

- What percentage of customers make a repeat purchase from you?

- What percentage of your service customers remain service customers, particularly when the product or item of equipment they have purchased from you runs out of its warranty period?

**Retention Rates**

Volvo enjoys a customer retention rate in excess of 70 per cent. Other, volume-orientated manufacturers are working hard to catch up!

**Cost of Gaining Customers**

How much does it cost you to gain a customer! Do you know?

An advertising agency can spend tens of thousands of pounds in making presentations to gain a new account. If it is successful in one presentation out of three, then the cost of gaining one new account is the cost of giving three presentations. This could exceed £100,000! Figures for a large advertising agency would be correspondingly higher.

We estimate that if you add together the rent, rates, heat, light, staffing, advertising, and other costs of running a new car showroom, it can cost £85 to get each prospective customer to walk into the showroom. If one customer in four buys a new car, the cost is $4 \times £85$, or £340.

It may not be easy, but can you divide your total costs of gaining customers by the number of new customers you gain?

**Saatchi & Saatchi**

In its statement of corporate philosophy, the famous advertising agency Saatchi & Saatchi writes about this:

'We want to grow – but most of all we want to grow with our existing clients. The new business won from an existing client is doubly rewarding – it means not only the increase in billings that comes with any new account, but also that you have strengthened a worthwhile relationship. (And, a track record of gaining more and more business from one existing client is in itself reassuring and attractive to potential new clients.) In every way, this seems to us the most desirable form of new business and we try to set the standard of service with this in mind.'

**Improving Your Profits**

The point is obvious. If it is very expensive to gain a new customer, then it is vitally important to retain as high a proportion of existing customers as possible.

Indeed, for many organisations, one easy way of improving profitability is to increase their customer-retention rate.

| Retention Index | In short, as noted before, you need to ensure that your monthly management accounting/information systems are extended to include customer-related indices. One of the key yardsticks you should use to evaluate the health of your business is: |
| --- | --- |

- your **customer-retention rate**.

I am pleased to say that due to the efforts of my colleagues our own retention index varies from month to month between 80 per cent and 90 per cent, with a mean average over many years of over 85 per cent. Moreover, we analyse very carefully the reasons for the missing 15 per cent. Most are due to retirement or the purchase of a small client by a larger client.

## CUSTOMER-RETAINING ACTIVITIES

| Carrot or Stick? | How do you set out to organise specific customer-retention activities? |
| --- | --- |

Is it either the carrot or the stick?

One company, penalises its sales team if they lose a customer by debiting them commission previously paid in respect of the business gained from that particular customer.

| Valued Customer Programmes | Some companies organise 'valued customer programmes'. |
| --- | --- |

Earlier we mentioned a company selling furniture by direct mail. This company uses its computerised customer database to send personal letters to valued customers, offering special concessions on repeat purchases and incentives if they can introduce new customers.

*Readers' Digest* does something similar when it gives concessionary prices to existing members who are willing to buy additional copies for friends or relatives.

| Customer Magazines/ Newsletters | Keeping in contact with your customers by a magazine or newsletter is important. |
| --- | --- |

It can be a real service to your customers to keep them abreast of modern developments. One computer software house enhanced its own reputation by developing a specialist magazine for the accounting profession and another for the legal profession.

Some of the company magazines and newsletters I see are so generalised as to be yet another 'give away'. It is important to use your

236

company magazine or newsletter to add value to the way in which you are perceived by the specific customers you seek to serve.

Austin-Rover produces a really valuable magazine for the owners of small businesses. Given that this is a particular **target** group of customers from which Austin-Rover wishes both to gain and retain business, this makes sense.

Customer Panels

There is a fair certainty that, among the hundreds of customers of your business, you have experts in a whole range of skills, including advertising, accountancy, personnel, property, promotions, and finance. In general, people love to be asked for their advice. Therefore, to form one or two 'customer panels' who meet periodically over dinner, or over a cheese and wine party, can be a worthwhile source of both customer goodwill and practical advice.

Customer Clubs

Given that you chose your customers because they had common interests, then clearly these common interests may make it possible for you to run a customer club, as we saw with Suzuki.

User Clubs

The higher the technology of your product or service, the more likely it is your customers will benefit by meeting other customers to exchange ideas on how to optimise the use of your product or service. The Grundfos Pumps Better Business Club is a good example.

Thus, if you know that your customers are facing common problems, you can generate goodwill, and additional business, setting out to find the experts who can solve these problems for them.

Social Evenings

One of the problems we all face as business executives is that the increasing pressures of competition mean we tend to work harder and harder, often to the detriment of our families.

If you can provide a social evening for families, then you can generate a considerable amount of goodwill which helps your subsequent relationships with customers.

## CUSTOMER FOLLOW-UP

Human Nature

Following up your customers is one of those mundane tasks which most sales departments know they should do, but which most sales departments neglect, despite the quite expensive systems which you have probably bought them to make the task easier!

237

| Constant Communication | As discussed earlier, it is vital to build up a complete customer database, not only of the customers who buy from you, but also all the people who at one time or another have expressed interest in becoming a customer. |
|---|---|

This technology must then be used to ensure that you keep in regular contact with your customers.

Your system is designed to establish how often each customer buys from you, and in what quantities, so that your sales team can **contact them** before they run out or buy their next purchase from a competitor.

| Customer Care | 'A customer rang H&J Quick subsidiary Trafford Vehicle Leasing – his car was parked at Manchester Airport, he had lost his keys in Paris and was flying to Dublin. Could they secure a new key ready for his return in two days' time? Stan spent some considerable time and effort in obtaining a hand-cut key (after being told by the manufacturer that they had to be specially cut by their laser cutting machine and that would take 7 days!), took it to the airport and left it for the driver to collect on his return from Dublin. Result . . . customer highly delighted!' |
|---|---|

*Photo shows Tim Worrall – Managing Director of the Quicks Group making the presentation to Stan Wright.*

## UPGRADING OUR PRODUCTS OR SERVICES

| Coca-Cola | Coca-Cola could be described as a fairly mundane brown fizzy drink. Moreover, it was a drink first formulated so long ago in 1890 that it should have been overtaken by the speed of progress and long forgotten. |
|---|---|

238

In fact, it is still a pre-eminent drink sustaining a multi-billion international business.

Why? The basic formula has remained virtually unchanged. So why has the drink survived so long?

Answer: the way in which the drink is presented to customers has been subject to constant change.

Millions have been spent in researching customer attitudes and expectations. The advertising has then been changed to reinforce these customer **perceptions** and attitudes.

It is a marvellous example of the need to constantly review the way in which we present our products and services to reconcile with the changing attitudes and perceptions of our customers.

# TEN STEP SUCCESS PLAN

Back to Basics

So, you and I cannot rest on our laurels. However successful we have been, we need to sustain that success by re-applying our Ten Step Plan.

Step One: Vision

If our original **vision** was sound, it should not need to be changed.

But, as we grow, as we take on more staff, or as staff change, we may well need to make sure our **vision** is still understood, and shared, by all those working in our company.

Step Two: Assess

We have seen industries undergo such a radical rationalisation as to be almost unrecognisable.

New technology, particularly electronics and computers, has both destroyed and created companies.

We have all experienced at first hand the dramatic changes in retailing.

It is necessary to study the potential of your market-place, and all the direct and indirect influences shaping its existing and future size and structure.

Step Three: Discover

Customers are changing. Long-established customers are retiring, or dying. New generations of customers have different beliefs and totally different life-styles. As a result, they have totally different needs and wants.

| | |
|---|---|
| Step Four:<br>Customer<br>Groupings | Customers can be compared to a kaleidoscope, constantly changing in new patterns. As we saw when we discussed this topic earlier, we used to sub-divide customers into socio-economic categories. Then Acorn sub-divided them by the types of houses in which they lived. More recently, it has been found far more accurate to group people by their life-styles. By the 1990s further refinements of the way in which we can sub-divide our customers will have emerged. |
| Step Five:<br>Target<br>Customers | All the preceding changes may present opportunities and threats, both to you and to your competitors. Are you in a position to exploit the opportunities better than your competitors? Can you avoid the threats better than your competitors? |
| | As the market-place becomes more competitive, and as your own company develops, you will need to make sure that you are building on strengths, while minimising your weaknesses. At the same time you need to have a realistic understanding of the strengths and weaknesses of your principal competitors. |
| | Against this SWOT analysis, are you still concentrating your efforts on those groups of customers whose similar needs and wants you can satisfy better than your competitors? Or do you need to re-focus your efforts on a different group of customers? |
| Step Six:<br>Mission | While your **vision** of total customer satisfaction may need little amendment, it is almost certain that your **mission statement** will need to be refined, if only because you now have a greater understanding of your industry, your customers, and – thus – the way in which you can better meet their needs. |
| | Moreover, enhanced technology may give you new tools to use in your drive for total customer satisfaction. |
| | It is a tribute to Simon Marks and his brother-in-law Israel Sieff that the six principles of business philosophy propounded by them in the early 1920s remain the basis of the philosophy of Marks and Spencer. |
| | But the wording of these principles has been changed, to reflect the technology of the 1980s. |
| Step Seven:<br>Create | My business has been going for 25 years. When we started, we were helping businesses to benefit from manual accounting systems. Today part of our work is to help them benefit from information technology, though this is only one element of a very much broader range of services. |

Doubtless, you have seen similar developments in the way in which you provide your product or service to your customers.

Both you and I need constantly to re-evaluate the following:

- the **design** of the product or services we provide
- the **channels** we use to reach our customers
- the **structure** we create within our own company to meet customer needs
- the **systems** we employ to meet customer needs.

Step Eight:
Attract

As we gain in experience, we evolve more cost-effective ways of attracting customers. I hope the alphabetical listing of the techniques we discussed under Step Eight will have helped to give you fresh ideas.

Step Nine:
Satisfy

It would be a healthy sign for British trade and industry if the concept we discussed of a **customer-satisfaction index** gains wider acceptance. It should certainly provide a stimulus for you and me to make sure that we constantly polish up and improve the ways in which we satisfy our customers.

Step Ten:
Retain

Finally, the circle is complete, and we are back to considering the importance of our **customer-retention index**.

## IN SEARCH OF EXCELLENCE

This was a marvellous title for a book which sums up the challenge of seeking to gain success in our business, or our professional practice, or even a social service with which we are connected.

I hope that our Ten Step Success Plan will help you in your drive to create excellence within your own organisation.

# BIBLIOGRAPHY

BENNIS Warren. *Planning of Change.* Holt 1985.

BRIGGS Asa. *Marks and Spencer 1884–1984.* Octopus Books Limited 1984.

CARLZON Jan. *Moments of Truth.* Ballinger Publishing Company 1987.

CLIFFORD Jr. Donald K and CAVANAGH Richard E. *The Winning Performance.* Bantam Books 1985.

DAVIDSON Hugh. *Offensive Marketing or How to make your competitors followers.* Penguin Books 1987.

DRUCKER Peter F. *Innovation and Entrepreneurship: practice and principles.* William Heinemann Ltd 1985.

GOLDSMITH Walter and CLUTTERBUCK David. *The Winning Streak.* Penguin Books 1985.

HARDY Len. *Successful Business Strategy.* Kogan Page 1987.

HICKMAN Craig R and SILVA Michael A. *Creating Excellence.* Allen and Unwin 1985.

McBURNIE Tony and CLUTTERBUCK David. *The Marketing Edge.* George Weidenfeld & Nicolson 1987.

McKAY Gilly and CORKE Alison. *The Body Shop: Franchising a Philosophy.* Pan Books Ltd 1987.

O'SHAUGNESSY John. *Competitive Marketing: A Strategic Approach.* Allen and Unwin 1985.

PETERS Tom and AUSTIN Nancy. *A Passion for Excellence.* Fontana Paperbacks 1986.

PETERS Thomas J and WATERMAN Jr Robert H. *In Search of Excellence.* Harper & Row 1982.

PILDITCH James. *Winning Ways: How 'Winning' Companies create the products we all want to buy.* Harper & Row Ltd 1987.

PORTER Michael E. *Competitive Advantage.* The Free Press 1985.

PORTER Michael E. *Competitive Strategy.* Collier Macmillan 1981.

REES Goronwy *St. Michael – History.* Pan 1979.

SCHMERTZ Herb and NOVAK William. *Goodbye to the Low Profile: The Art of Creative Confrontation.* Mercury Books 1986.

SEWELL R L. *Building A Business.* Pan Books 1986.

INDUSTRIAL MARKETING DIGEST is an excellent monthly publication which, as you will have seen by the many references to it, covers many of the topics in this book.

The address is: The Old Rectory, Ranmore Common, Dorking, Surrey RH5 6SP.

# INDEX